Charles Baudelaire

SELECTED POEMS

with translations by Geoffrey Wagner
and an introduction by Enid Starkie

Grove Press, Inc., New York

Copyright © 1974 by Geoffrey Wagner

All Rights Reserved

No part of this book may be reproduced, for any reason, by any means, including any method of photographic reproduction, without the permission of the publisher.

ISBN: 0-394-17831-9
Grove Press ISBN: 0-8021-0061-9

Library of Congress Catalog Card Number: 74-7679

First Evergreen Black Cat Edition 1974

9   8   7   6   5   4

Printed and bound in the United States of America

Distributed by Random House, Inc., New York

GROVE PRESS, INC.,
196 West Houston Street, New York, N.Y. 10014

Charles Baudelaire was born in 1821. His parents were moderately wealthy. Following the death of the poet's father the mother married an army general. The step-father seems to have been well-disposed to the boy but Baudelaire quit the family home for good as soon as the opportunity arose, taking his considerable paternal inheritance with him (he ran through half of it in two years). Thereafter he remained in touch only with his mother to whom he was always inordinately attached.

Baudelaire's France was a society in a state of flux. The old feudal order had been swept away, Napoleon's armies in their marches and counter-marches across Europe had opened up novel horizons, there was a restored (for a short time) but very bourgeois monarchy – and above all the industrial revolution was in full flood. It was an era of numerous options, and many artists were first confused, then disgusted, finally alienated. Authors began to write not for a popular market but for inner circles. Yet even in this context of cliques Baudelaire was still an outsider. After a short period of dandyism when he first arrived in Paris he devoted himself almost exclusively to the problems of his idiosyncratic private life – with earning as critic and reviewer enough to keep body and soul together, with exploring the dream worlds induced by opium, with his beautiful mulatto mistress, the famous (some would say infamous) Jeanne Duval, and before all else with the composition of his strikingly original poetry.

Baudelaire was a lyric poet to the manner born, and in this lies his final importance. Immediately, he was entranced by the day to day life of Paris, 'he was the first to see the beauty of the teeming modern city, to see beauty also in the dim little lives of those who inhabited these vast conglomerations' (Enid Starkie in the Introduction). Although this present selection of Baudelaire's poems concentrates chiefly on his erotic poetry nevertheless his 'metropolis' mind and instinct steadily show through. To say that the worthwhile poets of the last hundred years are indebted above all to Baudelaire's achievement is not too large a claim.

Bibliographical Notes

Baudelaire's collected poems (*Les Fleurs du mal*) were first published in 1857. The most satisfactory edition of his complete works was that of J. Crepet, published by Conrad in 1920. This selection concentrates chiefly on Baudelaire's erotic poetry, and includes some of the six poems banned as a result of Pinard's prosecution of 1857. Henri Peyre's long essay, 'Baudelaire as Love Poet', in the volume of that name (Yale University Press 1969) makes an admirable critical introduction to this side of Baudelaire's genius.

TABLE DES MATIERES

	page
L'Albatros	20
Correspondances	22
La Muse Vénale	24
La Vie Antérieure	26
La Géante	28
Parfum Exotique	30
La Chevelure	32
Sed Non Satiata	36
Avec ses vêtements ondoyants	38
Le Serpent qui Danse	40
Une Charogne	44
Le Chat	48
Un Fantôme: i. Le Parfum	50
Un Fantôme: ii. Le Cadre	52
Harmonie du Soir	54
Le Chat i	56
Le Chat ii	58
Le Beau Navire	60
Causerie	64
A Une Dame Créole	66
La Pipe	68
La Cloche Fêlée	70
Spleen	72
A Une Mendiante Rousse	74
A Une Passante	78
Le Crépuscule du Soir	80
Le Crépuscule du Matin	84
Une Martyre	86
Femmes Damnées	90
La Fin de la Journée	92
Le Voyage	94
Le Léthé	108
A Celle qui est Trop Gaie	110
Les Métamorphoses du Vampire	114
Les Yeux de Berthe	116
Hymne	118
Les Promesses d'un Visage	120
A Une Malabaraise	122
Recueillement	124
Les Plaintes d'un Icare	126

CONTENTS

The Albatross	*page* 21
Correspondences	23
The Mercenary Muse	25
Previous Existence	27
The Giantess	29
The Exotic Perfume	31
The Head of Hair	33
Sed Non Satiata	37
Sonnet	39
The Dancing Serpent	41
A Carrion	45
The Cat	49
A Ghost: i. Perfume	51
A Ghost: ii. The Frame	53
Evening Harmony	55
The Cat i	57
The Cat ii	59
The Beautiful Ship	61
Conversation	65
To a Creole Lady	67
The Pipe	69
The Cracked Bell	71
Spleen	73
To a Red-Haired Beggar Girl	75
To a Woman Passing By	79
Evening Twilight	81
Morning Twilight	85
A Martyred Woman	87
The Damned Women	91
The End of the Day	93
The Journey	95
Lethe	109
To Her Who is Too Gay	111
The Metamorphoses of the Vampire	115
The Eyes of My Child	117
Hymn	119
The Promises of a Face	121
To a Lady of Malabar	123
Meditation	125
The Lamentations of an Icarus	127

INTRODUCTION

FEW European poets are as widely read today as Charles Baudelaire and he has a special place in the affection of English readers, since Swinburne dedicated an obituary poem, *Ave Atque Vale*, to him in 1868, the year following his death.

Like most of the great French writers Baudelaire was born of middle-class parents. His father had been tutor to the family of Choiseul-Praslin before the French Revolution and occupied some post at the Senate under Napoleon until the Restoration. As a widower of sixty with an almost grown-up son he married a penniless orphan of twenty-five who could not hope for a better match and who was tired of living in a dependent position in the family of a friend of her father's. Charles, the only child of this marriage, was born two years later on 9th April, 1821. His father died when he was six and his mother married again, a fine soldier, a man of brains, courage and principle who had risen from the ranks under Napoleon and who was to become an ambassador and a Senator. In later life Baudelaire ascribed his unhappiness and the instability of his temperament to the fact of his mother's re-marriage. These psychological questions are however difficult to unravel. What is certain is that General Aupick was fond of his stepson, that he hoped much of him and that he treated him well according to his lights. But no one with a stern sense of discipline and responsibility would have been happy with the training of Baudelaire as a youth and the average father would probably have made no better job of it than the General. He had plans for Charles' future which the boy did not view with favour and he had the normal horror of the practical man for a literary career.

Charles did not show outstanding distinction at school. But, like many other famous French poets, he began his literary apprenticeship in the writing of original Latin verse and won a prize for his compositions. He left school when he had passed his 'baccalauréat' and then he embarked on vague academic studies in order to please his parents but secretly determined to practise writing. He did not spend a great deal of his time at his work and news of his escapades reached his family. To break what they considered evil connections they decided to send him on a trip to India with a friend of the General's, the captain of a ship bound for the East. The trip was to last twelve or fifteen months but Charles did not go any farther than Reunion. When the ship put in at Mauritius for repairs, after a bad storm, Charles, who was bored with his travelling companions, decided that nothing would induce him to proceed any farther, that he would return to France. At Mauritius he met literary people and fell, youthfully, in love with the wife of his host. He spent many happy days with his friends in the exotic scenery, filling his mind and imagination with dreams and images from which he was later to draw. It is this trip which made of him a poet and gave his poetry that peculiar nostalgic quality which we find in *La Vie antérieure*, *L'Invitation au Voyage*, *A une Dame créole* and other similar poems. He allowed himself to be persuaded to go as far as Reunion but there he transferred to the next boat returning to France.

On his return to France he reached his majority and he gained control of the capital which he had inherited under his father's will. He proceeded to live as the 'Jeunesse Dorée' had lived ten years before – Roger de Beauvoir and Barbey d'Aurevilly – and he rivalled the eccentricity of the *Bouzingos* of the 'thirties – Pétrus Borel and Philothée O'Neddy. His taste in literature was for the inspiration of horror, immorality and satanism of that period – the works of the Marquis de Sade, the *Contes Immoraux* of Pétrus Borel and the *Feu et*

Flamme of Philothée O'Neddy. The influence of these writings can be seen in his first compositions.

He began to write and composed then a large number of the *Fleurs du Mal*. The poems were largely those of a blasphemous and satanic nature – *Le Reniement de Saint Pierre* and *Les Litanies de Satan* – and the poems which show a love of horror and decay, like *Une Charogne*. He was already living with his octoroon mistress, the famous and infamous Jeanne Duval, for whom he wrote the poems of *Le Cycle de la Vénus noire*, the largest number of which were written during this period.

It was at this time that he established his reputation for eccentricity and unconventionality, and then most of the legends were invented.

This was the only really happy and carefree time of Baudelaire's life. We have as a record the charming happy painting by Deroy which is very different from the portraits and photographs which we know better, with the grim and tragic expression.

He was, however, squandering large sums of money and his family discovered that, in a couple of years, he had spent half his capital. A *Conseil Judiciaire* was appointed by law to administer his capital and to pay him only the interest monthly. Henceforth, for the rest of his life, Baudelaire was never to have more than small sums of money at his disposal. His life changed immediately and even his appearance. He gave up the rich and gaudy clothes and he was never again seen in anything but black broadcloth, though still of an original cut. His face gradually became set in the grim lines with which we are familiar. Then he began to experience the rigours of 'l'implacable vie'. He began to write the pessimistic poems, *La Cloche fêlée*, the *Spleen* poems and many others. Then he became a professional writer, trying to live by his pen, and he wrote the first of his famous aesthetic articles, the *Salons* of 1845 and 1846.

Having experienced poverty himself, Baudelaire became for a time imbued with revolutionary ideas and he played a small part in the Revolution of 1848. Then he made the acquaintance of the painter Courbet, who greatly influenced the realism of his writing and showed him the beauty of the contemporary scene. Baudelaire was one of the first and greatest of the poets to be inspired by the modern capital city, and these poems are amongst his greatest and most characteristic. He was the only poet of his time not to be impressed by the classical revival which he considered a 'pastiche inutile et dégoûtant'. He thought that the only artist who had any chance of survival was the one on whom his age had set its seal. 'Toute notre originalité vient de l'estampille que le temps imprime à nos sensations.' He was the first to see the beauty of the teeming modern city, to see beauty also in the dim little lives of those who inhabited these vast conglomerations. It was at this time that he composed *Crépuscule du Soir*. Then too, with a return of the venereal disease which he had thought cured, he wrote the tragic and bitter *Voyage à Cythère*.

Like the other writers who had taken part in it, Baudelaire was disgusted and discouraged with the outcome of the Revolution and fell into apathy and idleness. He was roused from this state by his discovery of the writings of the Swedish philosopher Swedenborg and the works of Edgar Allan Poe. When the seeds of this discovery began to bear fruit in the poems and articles after 1852, we reach the period of Baudelaire's maturity. The years from 1852 until the publication of *Les Fleurs du Mal* in 1857 are the most actively productive of his life. It is then he wrote the largest number of his greatest poems – *Bénédiction, Correspondances, Les Phares* and so forth – and also his most important articles of aesthetic criticism, not to mention his translations of the works of Poe which, if he had not reached a greater literary reputation in other fields, would have been sufficient to gain him an important place in French literature.

During this period Baudelaire's aesthetic articles should be read in conjunction with his poems, for it is difficult to separate the poet and the critic since poetry and criticism are two facets of his artistic nature, two aspects of the same experience. He considered all literary activity in the light of spiritual activity, an attempt to make concrete some transcendental experience. One expression of this experience was the crystallization – unconscious almost – in a poem. The other – conscious – was meditation on the nature of the experience and a discourse on the form in which it took place. Art was the reflection, the imperfect 'symbole' of eternal beauty and truth, and he held that it was impossible to imagine a great poet failing to be a critic as well. Otherwise he would remain an incomplete artist, a mere romantic poet inspired only by his instinct and his personal feelings. The poet is a translator of his experience into sounds, rhythms and images. The critic is also a translator – of another kind – a translator of his experience into meditation on its nature, into reflexion on its artistic crystallization. The critic must go beyond subjective 'translation', he must try to 'transformer sa volupté en connaissance' in order to reach a full understanding of art, beauty and even ultimate truth. An understanding of Baudelaire's critical works and an understanding of his aesthetic writings, an appreciation of the principles forming and underlying his judgments, lead to a fuller and deeper understanding of his poetry. His criticism is the key to his poetry and his poetry is an extension and fulfilment of his aesthetic doctrine. He believed that material objects exist in this world only because they have their origin in the world of the spirit. The hidden relation between things here below and in the world above he called – in Swedenborgian language – *Correspondances*. Everything in this world is merely the symbol of a hieroglyphic language and he claimed that it was the function of the artist to decipher the hidden writing of nature and to interpret the mysteries of the universe. He considered that only poets who had reached a high degree of spirituality were capable of understanding and interpreting these mysteries. Beauty was not for him, as it was for his contemporaries, material beauty alone. Beauty was essentially a spiritual reality and he was convinced that art was the greatest and perhaps the only means of effecting beauty in this world, art inspired by this mysterious and undying attraction of the ideal. For Baudelaire the search for beauty and the search for spiritual belief were the same thing and was the means of penetrating into the beyond and of translating its mysteries. Beauty for him did not lie in the subject itself but in what the artist brought to it. Beauty was the flame of the fire, the radiance of the energy, generated by the spiritual shock he received when he was moved and this spiritual shock could come from aspects hitherto considered ugly. He did not – as so many critics claim – see beauty in ugliness; he only said that from ugliness he could distil beauty. 'Tu m'as donné ta boue et j'en ai fait de l'or.' From the fire kindled in him the poet forged beauty and the intensity of the fire depended on his spiritual nature. The more spiritual the poet the greater the intensity of heat generated. Poetry for him was not mere composition and to be a poet meant to be capable of spiritual growth.

If this were merely a philosophical or religious belief it would not be so important in connection with Baudelaire's poetry. But he divined as well the use which could be made of these ideas in the realm of technique and this is one of the most original aspects of his art, the one which, more than anything else, tended to alter so radically French poetry at the end of the century. Since art in its totality reflects a vision, then each art – painting, music, sculpture and poetry – expresses in its own language, using its own hieroglyphics, what it has perceived in the realm where there are no boundaries, in the realm of pure beauty and truth. It follows thence that it matters little which artistic language is used to express the spiritual experience. Baudelaire imagined that it might be possible to find one art which would comprise all the languages, would appeal to all his senses 'fondus en un'. In his poetry he endeavoured to use the idiom of all the arts, to render what his eye saw not merely in line and colour, what his ear perceived not only in harmony, but to glide imperceptibly from one mode of expression to the other. Since 'les parfums, les couleurs et les sons se répondent' then he could render colour by means of harmony and sound by means of colour and line.

Inspired by these theories Baudelaire reached the full mastery and development of his art. At this time he not only wrote the spiritual poems mentioned earlier, but the evocative poems which are perhaps his highest artistic achievement – *L'Invitation au Voyage, Harmonie du Soir, La Vie antérieure* and many others. At this time also we have the second cycle of love poems, the *Cycle de la Vénus blanche*, poems of great symbolism and spiritual beauty, owing much to his new beliefs, a great contrast to the passionate and sensual inspiration of the *Cycle de la Vénus noire*.

The first version of *Les Fleurs du Mal* appeared in 1857 and Baudelaire hoped very much from the success of the book. Almost immediately it was arraigned by the public prosecutor on the charge of blasphemy and obscenity. The charge of blasphemy was dismissed but it was declared guilty of obscenity and the court ordered the excision of a number of poems before the volume could be circulated. Baudelaire refused to allow the book to be sold in its truncated form. He always claimed that his work was not a haphazard collection of poems, that it had an inner architecture and that the book was destroyed by omissions. He determined that he would replace the banned poems by others and that the second version be superior to the first. The second version appeared in 1861 and, although it lacks the banned poems, it is a greater work than the first. It is greater than the third version which, after his death, was augmented with every poem he had written added by his literary executors regardless of the plan.

The failure of the book on which he had counted so much was a great blow to Baudelaire, not only in the loss of the edition and the poems but also because he began to doubt the possibility of his own ultimate success as a writer. It coincided with the time of his breakdown in health. The chief characteristic of his writings for the rest of his life is deep pessimism and gloom, a deeper and more sincere pessimism than the pessimism of the *Spleen* poems of his youth. Amongst the thirty-five new poems of the second *Fleurs du Mal* – except two early poems which, for some reason, he did not include in the first version – the largest number give expression to weariness of life, to his horror at the swift flight of time, to the sensation of being carried away by a force greater than he, poems in the vein of *Chant d'Automne, Obsession, Le Goût du Néant* and *L'Horloge*. This version ended with the magnificent poem *Le Voyage*, worthy to be the coping stone of his work. Although it is not the last in chronological order it is likely that it would have remained the final poem of the third version which he was planning at the time when paralysis struck him down. Other poems were written after the publication of the second *Fleurs du Mal* of 1861; they are mostly further poems in the pessimistic vein – *Examen de Minuit, Le Gouffre* and *Plaintes d'un Icare*. But there is also the beautiful *Recueillement* written in a moment of resignation and *L'Avertisseur* which expresses hope of salvation.

The second version of *Les Fleurs du Mal* did not prove more fortunate than the first. The publisher, Poulet Malassis, went bankrupt in 1862 before the edition was sold out and fled to Belgium to escape his creditors. All his stock was sold for little more than the paper on which it was printed.

In an effort to retrieve his fortunes Baudelaire went to Belgium in 1864 on a lecturing tour. Brussels had an active literary life at that time for there were living there many French writers who had gone into exile during the Second Empire. His lectures were, however, a failure and his writings were no better understood or appreciated in Belgium than they were in France. Pride prevented him from returning to Paris until his fortunes had taken a turn for the better. During his exile in Brussels he was trying to negotiate a contract with publishers – both in Belgium and in France – for an edition of his works. He could have secured publication of his poems but he did not wish to separate them from the rest of his work. He considered that his critical writings were of great importance and he wished them to appear, with his poems, in a uniform edition. Before he had been able to sign a contract he was struck down by paralysis as he was visiting the cathedral at Namur.

As soon as he recovered partial use of his limbs he was brought back to Paris but he never regained the power of speech. It is said that he kept his intellectual powers to the end and that he became converted in his last months. It is, however, difficult to speak with certainty of the death-bed conversion of a paralysed man incapable of speech and maybe incapable also of lucid thought.

He died peacefully on 31st August, 1867, during the summer holidays when Paris was almost empty. Only a thin stream of mourners followed the coffin to the cemetery of Montparnasse where he lies buried in the same grave as his stepfather. The *Société des Gens de Lettres* sent no representative to the funeral and the absence of many close friends was noticed – Sainte-Beuve, whom Baudelaire had so greatly liked and admired, and Gautier to whom he had dedicated his *Fleurs du Mal*. The same neglect and indifference which had dogged his literary career followed him to the grave. Only two speeches were delivered at the graveside, by two friends of long standing – Banville and Asselineau – and these were pledges of friendship rather than literary tributes. One writer, a young poet who had never met him, realized the significance of the passing. This was Paul Verlaine who, the previous year, at the age of twenty-two, had published his first book of poems, *Poèmes Saturniens*, which owe much to Baudelaire's influence and who, at the age of twenty-one, had written in *L'Art* the most sensitive criticism of his poetry which appeared during the lifetime of the poet.

Baudelaire's works – published and unpublished – were put up to auction and Lévy secured the rights on them for £70 until the copyright expired fifty years later.

During the seventy odd years which have elapsed since his death the works of Baudelaire have enjoyed several different and distinct vogues. After the defeat of France in the Franco-Prussian War, when the country turned in revulsion against all aspects of the Second Empire, when the writers were seeking something new with which to replace the outworn fashion of *Le Parnasse*, then they discovered the poet who had been so much misunderstood and neglected during the previous period and drew inspiration from his works. They seized on his poem *Correspondances*, making of it the manifesto of the new movement, while his conception of *le symbole* gave its name to their school of poetry, *Le Symbolisme*. They admired in him the sensuous poet of rare sensations, who had wished in his poetry to emulate the evocative power of music, and, thinking they were following him, they tried to take over – often with disastrous results – the means of expression of music. But they largely copied the poems of decay and horror of the early years. They saw Baudelaire chiefly as a Dandy, an aesthete, a decadent, a man who blasphemed against accepted religion and morality, who smoked opium and hashish, who was said to dabble in Satanism and to practise all manner of vice and corruption. Des Esseintes, the hero of Huysmans' novel *A Rebours*, is typical of the Baudelairian character of the day and he was copied by many writers and men of fashion. This novel is the 'yellow-back' which helps Dorian Gray on his way to perdition in Oscar Wilde's novel of that name. In the 'eighties and 'nineties the Baudelaire influence came to be identified with everything which was morbid, decadent and immoral. There were many aspects of his work which they did not appreciate and which they would not have understood.

During the early years of the twentieth century his influence waned. Then the fashion was for internationalism, for mass movements, for the brotherhood of man, for boundless energy and naïve effort. The war of 1914 showed up the hollowness of all these illusions and with the coming of peace, when his copyright expired and the editions of his works multiplied, he enjoyed a new vogue. Then it was the poet of sensuous pleasure who was admired and also the poet who was disillusioned and often cynical. Baudelaire seemed to them also the poet who could best express modern man, the product of all the revolutions – political, social and industrial. No other poet seemed to have been aware of these problems in so sensitive a manner. Later, as the years of peace progressed, and the aridity of the pursuit of pleasure and material comfort became apparent, many found an echo in Baudelaire of their disgusts and disappointments. He had said that these things did not constitute happiness and progress, that true progress consisted in improving man's evil nature. As dictatorships sprang up and individual human values vanished they found comfort in his revolt against the denial of the supreme importance of each individual human soul and its enslavement to machine or state. Then also the spiritual aspect of his work – hitherto unnoticed – was appreciated and it was seen that he was seeking what most thinking human beings seek today, a remedy to their despairs and disillusionments. The Catholics seized on him as their chosen poet and went too far in their efforts to make of him a genuine Catholic and, in so doing, were forced to neglect and overlook – or misinterpret – a large part of his work. It is true that if Baudelaire's writings are studied with regard to the chronological order it becomes apparent that, after he reached maturity, the chief of his preoccupations was for spiritual values, a hunger and thirst for spiritual food. He used to say that he was bored in France because everyone was like

Voltaire. It is true that the problem of sin never ceased to preoccupy him and that his expression of remorse has a truly Catholic ring, that his work is based on the duality of the conflict in man, between *Spleen* and *Idéal*, between his idealistic aspirations and his sinful nature. But it is difficult to call truly Catholic a poet who – except in his rebellious youth and then only in blasphemy – took no account of Christ or the Redemption. He was obsessed by the irreparableness of the past, by the knowledge that what was done could never now be undone.

> *L'Irréparable ronge avec sa dent maudite*
> *Notre âme, piteux monument.*

He was guilty of the sins of intellectual pride and despair and these are grievous sins in Catholic doctrine.

Baudelaire is certainly a poet of great variety and complexity and this explains the diversity of opinions which have been expressed about him, so that he could, on the one hand, be considered as symbolical of everything that was corrupt and evil, and, on the other, one of the great spiritual poets. He is a poet of subtle and rare sensation, a poet of great evocative and suggestive power and at the same time a poet of realism who was aware of the commonplace and ordinary. He is one of the great love poets of France, a poet of sensual passion which he has expressed with the magnificence of the *Song of Solomon*, and also a poet of the purest spiritual love. In some poems he has turned his thoughts towards religious and metaphysical aspiration and in others towards social and psychological problems which are still ours today. And finally he is a poet whose best poems have the classical perfection of style of the *Grand Siècle*.

ENID STARKIE

L'ALBATROS

SOUVENT, pour s'amuser, les hommes d'équipage
Prennent des albatros, vastes oiseaus des mers,
Qui suivent, indolents compagnons de voyage,
Le navire glissant sur les gouffres amers.

A peine les ont-ils déposés sur les planches,
Que ces rois de l'azur, maladroits et honteux,
Laissent piteusement leurs grandes ailes blanches
Comme des avirons traîner a côté d'eux.

Ce voyageur ailé, comme il est gauche et veule!
Lui, naguère si beau, qu'il est comique et laid!
L'un agace son bec avec un brûle-gueule,
L'autre mime, en boitant, l'infirme qui volait!

Le Poëte est semblable au prince des nuées
Qui hante la tempête et se rit de l'archer;
Exilé sur le sol au milieu des huées,
Ses ailes de géant l'empêchent de marcher.

THE ALBATROSS

OFTEN, to amuse themselves, the men of the crew
　　Catch those great birds of the seas, the albatrosses,
Lazy companions of the voyage, who follow
The ship that slips through bitter gulfs.

Hardly have they put them on the deck,
Than these kings of the skies, awkward and ashamed,
Piteously let their great white wings
Draggle like oars beside them.

This winged traveller, how weak he becomes and slack!
He who of late was so beautiful, how comical and ugly!
Someone teases his beak with a branding iron,
Another mimics, limping, the crippled flyer!

The Poet is like the prince of the clouds,
Haunting the tempest and laughing at the archer;
Exiled on earth amongst the shouting people,
His giant's wings hinder him from walking.

CORRESPONDANCES

LA Nature est un temple où de vivants piliers
Laissent parfois sortir de confuses paroles;
L'homme y passe à travers des forêts de symboles
Qui l'observent avec des regards familiers.

Comme de longs échos qui de loin se confondent
Dans une ténébreuse et profonde unité,
Vaste comme la nuit et comme la clarté,
Les parfums, les couleurs et les sons se répondent.

Il est des parfums frais comme des chairs d'enfants,
Doux comme les hautbois, verts comme les prairies,
Et d'autres, corrompus, riches et triomphants,

Ayant l'expansion des choses infinies,
Comme l'ambre, le musc, le benjoin et l'encens,
Qui chantent les transports de l'esprit et des sens.

CORRESPONDENCES

NATURE is a temple where living pillars
   Let sometimes emerge confused words;
Man crosses it through forests of symbols
Which watch him with intimate eyes.

Like those deep echoes that meet from afar
In a dark and profound harmony,
As vast as night and clarity,
So perfumes, colours, tones answer each other.

There are perfumes fresh as children's flesh,
Soft as oboes, green as meadows,
And others, corrupted, rich, triumphant,

Possessing the diffusion of infinite things,
Like amber, musk, incense and aromatic resin,
Chanting the ecstasies of spirit and senses.

LA MUSE VENALE

O MUSE de mon cœur, amante des palais,
  Auras-tu, quand Janvier lâchera ses Borées,
Durant les noirs ennuis des neigeuses soirées,
Un tison pour chauffer tes deux pieds violets?

Ranimeras-tu donc tes épaules marbrées
Aus nocturnes rayons qui percent les volets?
Sentant ta bourse à sec autant que ton palais,
Récolteras-tu l'or des voûtes azurées?

Il te faut, pour gagner ton pain de chaque soir,
Comme un enfant de chœur, jouer de l'encensoir,
Chanter des *Te Deum* auxquels tu ne crois guère,

Ou, saltimbanque à jeun, étaler tes appas
Et ton rire trempé de pleurs qu'on ne voit pas,
Pour faire épanouir la rate du vulgaire.

THE MERCENARY MUSE

O MUSE of my heart, votary of palaces,
  Shall you, when January looses its boreal winds,
Have any firebrand to warm your violet feet
In the black boredoms of snowy evenings?

Shall you revive your marble shoulders
By the gleams of night that stab the shutters?
And, feeling your purse as empty as your palace,
Will you reap the gold of azure skies?

To win your evening bread you need,
Like a choir-boy, to play with the censer,
To chant the Te Deums you scarcely believe in,

Or, famished vagabond, expose your charms
And your laughter soaked in crying that is not seen,
In order to dispel the spleen of the people.

LA VIE ANTERIEURE

J'AI longtemps habité sous de vastes portiques
   Que les soleils marins teignaient de mille feux,
Et que leurs grands piliers, droits et majestueux,
Rendaient pareils, le soir, aux grottes basaltiques.

Les houles, en roulant les images des cieux,
Mêlaient d'une façon solennelle et mystique
Les tout-puissants accords de leur riche musique
Aux couleurs du couchant reflété par mes yeux.

C'est là que j'ai vécu dans les voluptés calmes,
Au milieu de l'azur, des vagues, des splendeurs
Et des esclaves nus, tout imprégnés d'odeurs,

Qui me rafraîchissaient le front avec des palmes,
Et dont l'unique soin était d'approfondir
Le secret douloureux qui me faisait languir.

PREVIOUS EXISTENCE

FOR a long time I lived under vast colonnades,
   Stained with a thousand fires by ocean suns,
Whose vast pillars, straight and majestic,
Made them seem in the evening like grottos of basalt.

The sea-swells, in swaying the pictures of the skies,
Mingled solemnly and mystically
The all-powerful harmonies of their rich music
With the colours of the setting sun reflected by my eyes.

It is there that I have lived in calm voluptuousness,
In the centre of the blue, amidst the waves and splendours
And the nude slaves, heavy with perfumes,

Who refreshed my forehead with palm-leaves,
Their only care was to fathom
The dolorous secret that made me languish.

LA GÉANTE

Du temps que la Nature en sa verve puissante
   Concevait chaque jour des enfants monstrueux,
J'eusse aimé vivre auprès d'une jeune géante,
Comme aux pieds d'une reine un chat voluptueux.

J'eusse aimé voir son corps fleurir avec son âme
Et grandir librement dans ses terribles jeux;
Deviner si son cœur couve une sombre flamme
Aux humides brouillards qui nagent dans ses yeux;

Parcourir à loisir ses magnifiques formes;
Ramper sur le versant de ses genoux énormes,
Et parfois en été, quand les soleils malsains,

Lasse, la font s'étendre à travers la campagne,
Dormir nonchalamment à l'ombre de ses seins,
Comme un hameau paisible au pied d'une montagne.

THE GIANTESS

IN those times when Nature in powerful zest
Conceived each day monstrous children,
I would have loved to live near a young giantess,
A voluptuous cat at the feet of a queen.

I would have loved to see her body flower with her soul,
To grow up freely in her prodigious play;
To find if her heart bred some dark flame
Amongst the humid mists swimming in her eyes;

To run leisurely over her marvellous lines;
To creep along the slopes of her enormous knees,
And sometimes in summer, when impure suns

Made her wearily stretch out across the countryside,
To sleep carelessly in the shadow of her breasts,
Like a peaceful village at the foot of a mountain.

PARFUM EXOTIQUE

Quand, les deux yeux fermés, en un soir chaud
    d'automne,
Je respire l'odeur de ton sein chaleureux,
Je vois se dérouler des rivages heureux
Qu'éblouissent les feux d'un soleil monotone;

Une île paresseuse où la nature donne
Des arbres singuliers et des fruits savoureux;
Des hommes dont le corps est mince et vigoureux,
Et des femmes dont l'œil par sa franchise étonne.

Guidé par ton odeur vers de charmants climats,
Je vois un port rempli de voiles et de mâts
Encore tout fatigués par la vague marine,

Pendant que le parfum des verts tamariniers,
Qui circule dans l'air et m'enfle la narine,
Se mêle dans mon âme au chant des mariniers.

THE EXOTIC PERFUME

WHEN, with both eyes shut, on a close autumn evening,
I breathe the perfume of your heated breast,
I see happy shores unfold themselves
Dazzling in the flames of a monotonous sun;

A lazy island where Nature bestows
Peculiar trees and savoury fruit;
Men with bodies slim and virile,
Women with eyes of astonishing candour.

Led by your odour to climates of charm,
I see a harbour full of sails and masts
Still tired by the waves of the sea,

Whilst the perfume of green tamarind-trees
Circles the air and fills my nostrils,
Meets in my soul with the song of the seamen.

LA CHEVELURE

O TOISON, moutonnant jusque sur l'encolure!
O boucles! O parfum chargé de nonchaloir!
Extase! Pour peupler ce soir l'alcôve obscure
Des souvenirs dormant dans cette chevelure,
Je la veux agiter dans l'air comme un mouchoir!

La langoureuse Asie et la brûlante Afrique,
Tout un monde lointain, absent, presque défunt,
Vit dans tes profondeurs, forêt aromatique!
Comme d'autres esprits voguent sur la musique,
Le mien, ô mon amour! nage sur ton parfum.

J'irai là-bas où l'arbre et l'homme, pleins de sève,
Se pâment longuement sous l'ardeur des climats;
Fortes tresses, soyez la houle qui m'enlève!
Tu contiens, mer d'ébène, un éblouissant rêve
De voiles, de rameurs, de flammes et de mâts:

Un port retentissant où mon âme peut boire
A grands flots le parfum, le son et la couleur;
Où les vaisseaux, glissant dans l'or et dans la moire,
Ouvrent leurs vastes bras pour embrasser la gloire
D'un ciel pur où frémit l'éternelle chaleur.

Je plongerai ma tête amoureuse d'ivresse
Dans ce noir océan où l'autre est enfermé;
Et mon esprit subtil que le roulis caresse
Saura vous retrouver, ô féconde paresse!
Infinis bercements du loisir embaumé!

THE HEAD OF HAIR

O FLEECE, foaming to the neck!
O curls! O scent of laziness!
Ecstasy! This evening, to people the dark corners
Of memories that are sleeping in these locks,
I would wave them in the air like a handkerchief!

Languorous Asia and burning Africa,
A whole world, distant, absent, almost extinct,
Lives in the depths of your perfumed jungle;
As other souls sail along on music,
So mine, O my love, swims on your scent.

I shall go over there where trees and men, full of sap,
Faint away slowly in the passionate climate;
O strong locks, be the sea-swell that transports me!
You keep, O sea of ebony, a dazzling dream
Of sails and sailormen, flames and masts:

A resounding haven where in great waves
My soul can drink the scent, the sound and colour;
Where ships, sliding in gold and watered silk,
Part their vast arms to embrace the glory
Of the pure sky shuddering with eternal heat

I shall plunge my head, adoring drunkenness,
Into this black ocean where the other is imprisoned;
And my subtle spirit caressed by the sway
Will know how to find you, O pregnant idleness!
In an infinite cradle of scented leisure!

Cheveux bleus, pavillon de ténèbres tendues,
Vous me rendez l'azur du ciel immense et rond;
Sur les bords duvetés de vos mèches tordues
Je m'enivre ardemment des senteurs confondues
De l'huile de coco, du musc et du goudron.

Longtemps! toujours! ma main dans ta crinière lourde
Sèmera le rubis, la perle et le saphir,
Afin qu'à mon désir tu ne sois jamais sourde!
N'es-tu pas l'oasis où je rêve, et la gourde
Où je hume à longs traits le vin du souvenir?

Blue hair, house of taut darkness,
You make the blue of the sky seem huge and round for me;
On the downy edges of your twisted locks
I hungrily get drunk on the muddled fragrances
Of coconut oil, of musk and tar

For a long time! For ever! Amongst your heavy mane
My hand will strew the ruby, pearl and sapphire
To make you never deaf to my desire!
For are you not the oasis where I dream, the gourd
Where in great draughts I gulp the wine of memory?

SED NON SATIATA

BIZARRE déité, brune comme les nuits,
   Au parfum mélangé de musc et de havane,
Œuvre de quelque obi, le Faust de la savane,
Sorcière au flanc d'ébène, enfant des noirs minuits,

Je préfère au constance, à l'opium, au nuits,
L'élixir de ta bouche où l'amour se pavane;
Quand vers toi mes désirs partent en caravane,
Tes yeux sont la citerne où boivent mes ennuis.

Par ces deux grands yeux noirs, soupiraux de ton âme,
O démon sans pitié! verse-moi moins de flamme;
Je ne suis pas le Styx pour t'embrasser neuf fois,

Hélas! et je ne puis, Mégère libertine,
Pour briser ton courage et te mettre aux abois,
Dans l'enfer de ton lit devenir Proserpine!

SED NON SATIATA

Strange deity, brown as nights,
  Whose perfume is mixed with musk and Havanah,
Magical creation, Faust of the savanna,
Sorceress with the ebony thighs, child of black midnights,

I prefer to African wines, to opium, to burgundy,
The elixir of your mouth where love parades itself;
When my desires leave in caravan for you,
Your eyes are the reservoir where my cares drink.

From those two great black eyes, chimneys of our spirit,
O pitiless demon, throw out less flame at me;
I am no Styx to clasp you nine times,

Nor can I, alas, dissolute shrew,
To break your courage, bring you to bay,
Become any Proserpine in the hell of your bed!

AVEC SES VÊTEMENTS

AVEC ses vêtements ondoyants et nacrés,
  Même quand elle marche, on croirait qu'elle danse,
Comme ces longs serpents que les jongleurs sacrés
Au bout de leurs bâtons agitent en cadence.

Comme le sable morne et l'azur des déserts,
Insensibles tous deux à l'humaine souffrance,
Comme les longs réseaux de la houle des mers,
Elle se développe avec indifférence.

Ses yeux polis sont faits de minéraux charmants,
Et dans cette nature étrange et symbolique
Où l'ange inviolé se mêle au sphinx antique,

Où tout n'est qu'or, acier, lumière et diamants,
Resplendit à jamais, comme un astre inutile,
La froide majesté de la femme stérile.

SONNET

WITH her dresses undulating, pearly,
    Even walking one would think her dancing,
Like those long serpents which holy charmers
Move in harmony at the tips of their batons.

Like the dull sand and the blue of deserts,
Unmoved alike by human pain,
Like the long fabric of the swell of seas,
She unfolds herself with indifference.

Her polished eyes are of delicious metals,
And in this strange, symbolic nature
Where virgin angel meets with ancient sphinx,

Where all is only gold and steel and light and diamonds,
There shines for ever, like a useless star,
The cold majesty of the sterile woman.

LE SERPENT QUI DANSE

QUE j'aime voir, chère indolente,
　　De ton corps si beau,
Comme une étoffe vacillante,
　　Miroiter la peau!

Sur ta chevelure profonde
　　Aux âcres parfums,
Mer odorante et vagabonde
　　Aux flots bleus et bruns,

Comme un navire qui s'éveille
　　Au vent du matin,
Mon âme rêveuse appareille
　　Pour un ciel lointain.

Tes yeux, où rien ne se révèle
　　De doux ni d'amer,
Sont deux bijoux froids où se mêle
　　L'or avec le fer.

A te voir marcher en cadence,
　　Belle d'abandon,
On dirait un serpent qui danse
　　Au bout d'un bâton.

Sous le fardeau de ta paresse
　　Ta tête d'enfant
Se balance avec la mollesse
　　D'un jeune éléphant,

Et ton corps se penche et s'allonge
　　Comme un fin vaisseau
Qui roule bord sur bord et plonge
　　Ses vergues dan l'eau.

page 40

THE DANCING SERPENT

HOW I love to watch, dear indolent creature,
   The skin of your so
Beautiful body glisten, like some
   Quivering material!

On your deep coiffure
   Bitter scented,
Scented, restless sea,
   With the blue and brown waves,

Like a ship waking
   To the wind of morning,
My dreamy soul prepares
   For skies far away.

Your eyes, where nothing is revealed
   Of sweet or sour,
Are two cold gems whose gold
   Is mixed with iron.

Seeing your harmonious walk,
   Abandoned beauty,
One would say a snake was dancing
   At the end of a stick.

Under the weight of your sloth
   Your infant head
Is balanced with the indolence
   Of a young elephant,

And your body bends and stretches
   Like a delicate ship
Pitching from side to side and sinking
   Its spars in the water.

Comme un flot grossi par la fonte
　　Des glaciers grondants,
Quand l'eau de ta bouche remonte
　　Au bord de tes dents,

Je crois boire un vin de Bohême,
　　Amer et vainqueur,
Un ciel liquide qui parsème
　　D'étoiles mon cœur!

Like a wave swelled by the melting
   Of a groaning glacier,
When your saliva rises
   To the edges of your teeth,

I feel I drink some Bohemian wine,
   Bitter, victor,
A liquid sky that scatters
   Stars in my heart!

UNE CHAROGNE

RAPPELEZ-VOUS l'objet que nous vîmes, mon âme,
   Ce beau matin d'été si doux:
Au détour d'un sentier une charogne infâme
   Sur un lit semé de cailloux,

Les jambes en l'air, comme une femme lubrique,
   Brûlante et suant les poisons,
Ouvrait d'une façon nonchalante et cynique
   Son ventre plein d'exhalaisons.

Le soleil rayonnait sur cette pourriture,
   Comme afin de la cuire à point,
Et de rendre au centuple à la grande Nature
   Tout ce qu'ensemble elle avait joint;

Et le ciel regardait la carcasse superbe
   Comme une fleur s'épanouir.
La puanteur était si forte, que sur l'herbe
   Vous crûtes vous évanouir.

Les mouches bourdonnaient sur ce ventre putride,
   D'où sortaient de noirs bataillons
De larves, qui coulaient comme un épais liquide
   Le long de ces vivants haillons.

Tout cela descendait, montait comme une vague,
   Ou s'élançait en pétillant;
On eût dit que le corps, enflé d'un souffle vague,
   Vivait en se multipliant.

Et ce monde rendait une étrange musique,
   Comme l'eau courante et le vent,
Ou le grain qu'un vanneur d'un mouvement rhythmique
   Agite et tourne dans son van.

A CARRION

Do you remember the thing we saw, my soul,
  That summer morning, so beautiful, so soft:
At a turning in the path, a filthy carrion,
  On a bed sown with stones,

Legs in the air, like a lascivious woman,
  Burning and sweating poisons,
Opened carelessly, cynically,
  Its great fetid belly.

The sun shone on this fester,
  As though to cook it to a turn,
And to return a hundredfold to great Nature
  What she had joined in one;

And the sky saw the superb carcase
  Open like a flower.
The stench was so strong, that you might think
  To swoon away upon the grass.

The flies swarmed on that rotten belly,
  Whence came out black battalions
Of spawn, flowing like a thick liquid
  Along its living tatters.

All this rose and fell like a wave,
  Or rustled in jerks;
One would have said that the body, full of a loose breath,
  Lived in this its procreation.

And this world gave out a strange music,
  Like flowing water and wind,
Or a winnower's grain that he shakes and turns
  With rhythmical grace in his basket.

Les formes s'effaçaient et n'étaient plus qu'un rêve,
  Une ébauche lente à venir
Sur la toile oubliée, et que l'artiste achève
  Seulement par le souvenir.

Derrière les rochers une chienne inquiète
  Nous regardait d'un œil fâché,
Epiant le moment de reprendre au squelette
  Le morceau qu'elle avait lâché.

—Et pourtant vous serez semblable à cette ordure,
  A cette horrible infection,
Etoile de mes yeux, soleil de ma nature,
  Vous, mon ange et ma passion!

Oui! telle vous serez, ô la reine des grâces,
  Après les derniers sacrements,
Quand vous irez, sous l'herbe et les floraisons grasses,
  Moisir parmi les ossements.

Alors, ô ma beauté! dites à la vermine
  Qui vous mangera de baisers,
Que j'ai gardé la forme et l'essence divine
  De mes amours décomposés!

The forms fade and are no more than a dream,
   A sketch slow to come
On the forgotten canvas, and that the artist completes
   Only by memory.

Behind the boulders an anxious bitch
   Watched us with angry eyes,
Spying the moment to regain in the skeleton
   The morsel she had dropped.

—And yet you will be like this excrement,
   This horrible stench,
O star of my eyes, sun of my being,
   You, my angel, my passion.

Yes, such you will be, queen of gracefulness,
   After the last sacraments,
When you go beneath the grasses and fat flowers,
   Mouldering amongst the bones.

Then, my beauty, say to the vermin
   Which will eat you with kisses,
That I have kept the shape and the divine substance
   Of my decomposed loves!

LE CHAT

VIENS, mon beau chat, sur mon cœur amoureux;
  Retiens les griffes de ta patte,
Et laisse-moi plonger dans tes beaux yeux,
  Mêlés de métal et d'agate.

Lorsque mes doigts caressent à loisir
  Ta tête et ton dos élastique,
Et que ma main s'enivre du plaisir
  De palper ton corps électrique,

Je vois ma femme en esprit.   Son regard,
  Comme le tien, aimable bête,
Profond et froid, coupe et fend comme un dard,

Et, des pieds jusques à la tête,
  Un air subtil, un dangereux parfum,
Nagent autour de son corps brun.

THE CAT

MY beautiful cat, come onto my heart full of love;
   Hold back the claws of your paw,
And let me plunge into your adorable eyes
   Mixed with metal and agate.

When my fingers lazily fondle
   Your head and your elastic back,
And my hand gets drunk with the pleasure
   Of feeling your electric body,

I see in spirit my personal lady. Her glance,
   Like yours, dear creature,
Deep and cold, slits and splits like a dart,

And from her feet to her head,
   A subtle atmosphere, a dangerous perfume,
Swim around her brown body.

UN FANTOME

i. Le Parfum

LECTEUR, as-tu quelquefois respiré
Avec ivresse et lente gourmandise
Ce grain d'encens qui remplit une église,
Ou d'un sachet le musc invétéré?

Charme profond, magique, dont nous grise
Dans le présent le passé restauré!
Ainsi l'amant sur un corps adoré
Du souvenir cueille la fleur exquise.

De ses cheveux élastiques et lourds,
Vivant sachet, encensoir de l'alcôve,
Une senteur montait, sauvage et fauve,

Et des habits, mousseline ou velours,
Tout imprégnés de sa jeunesse pure,
Se dégageait un parfum de fourrure.

A GHOST

i. Perfume

READER, have you ever breathed in
With intoxication and slow gluttony,
That grain of incense which fills a church,
Or that embedded musk of a scent-bag?

Deep, magical charm, the past recalled
By you now makes us drunk.
Thus a lover plucks from an adored body
The exquisite flower of memory.

From her buoyant, heavy hair,
A living sachet, censer of recesses,
There climbs a fragrance, savage, wild,

And from her muslin or velvet dresses,
Permeated with her pure youth,
Escapes a perfume of fur.

ii. Le Cadre

COMME un beau cadre ajoute à la peinture,
  Bien qu'elle soit d'un pinceau très-vanté,
Je ne sais quoi d'étrange et d'enchanté
En l'isolant de l'immense nature,

Ainsi bijoux, meubles, métaux, dorure,
S'adaptaient juste à sa rare beauté;
Rien n'offusquait sa parfaite clarté,
Et tout semblait lui servir de bordure.

Même on eût dit parfois qu'elle croyait
Que tout voulait l'aimer; elle noyait
Sa nudité voluptueusement

Dans les baisers du satin et du linge,
Et, lente ou brusque, à chaque mouvement
Montrait la grâce enfantine du singe.

ii. The Frame

AS a fine frame adds to its picture,
   Though it may come from a well-known brush,
Thus jewels, furniture, metals or gilding
Adapted themselves quite to her unusual beauty;

It was some strange enchantment,
Parting her from enormous nature;
Nothing darkened her perfect pellucidity,
Everything seemed to serve her as frame.

At times one would even have said that she thought
That all things desired to love her; voluptuously
She drowned her nakedness

In kisses of satin and linen,
And, slow or sudden, in each movement
Showed the childlike grace of the monkey.

HARMONIE DU SOIR

VOICI venir les temps où vibrant sur sa tige
    Chaque fleur s'évapore ainsi qu'un encensoir;
Les sons et les parfums tournent dans l'air du soir;
Valse mélancolique et langoureux vertige!

Chaque fleur s'évapore ainsi qu'un encensoir;
Le violon frémit comme un cœur qu'on afflige;
Valse mélancolique et langoureux vertige!
Le ciel est triste et beau comme un grand reposoir.

Le violon frémit comme un cœur qu'on afflige,
Un cœur tendre, qui hait le néant vaste et noir!
Le ciel est triste et beau comme un grand reposoir;
Le soleil s'est noyé dans son sang qui se fige.

Un cœur tendre, qui hait le néant vaste et noir,
Du passé lumineux recueille tout vestige!
Le soleil s'est noyé dans son sang qui se fige.
Ton souvenir en moi luit comme un ostensoir!

EVENING HARMONY

NOW is the time when trembling on its stem
    Each flower fades away like incense;
Sounds and scents turn in the evening air;
A melancholy waltz, a soft and giddy dizziness!

Each flower fades away like incense;
The violin thrills like a tortured heart;
A melancholy waltz, a soft and giddy dizziness!
The sky is sad and beautiful like some great resting-place.

The violin thrills like a tortured heart,
A tender heart, hating the wide black void.
The sky is sad and beautiful like some great resting-place;
The sun drowns itself in its own clotting blood.

A tender heart, hating the wide black void,
Gathers all trace from the pellucid past.
The sun drowns itself in clotting blood.
Like the Host shines O your memory in me!

LE CHAT

I

Dans ma cervelle se promène,
    Ainsi qu'en son appartement,
Un beau chat, fort, doux et charmant.
Quand il miaule, on l'entend à peine,

Tant son timbre est tendre et discret;
Mais que sa voix s'apaise ou gronde,
Elle est toujours riche et profonde:
C'est là son charme et son secret.

Cette voix, qui perle et qui filtre
Dans mon fond le plus ténébreux,
Me remplit comme un vers nombreux
Et me réjouit comme un philtre.

Elle endort les plus cruels maux
Et contient toutes les extases;
Pour dire les plus longues phrases,
Elle n'a pas besoin de mots.

Non, il n'est pas d'archet qui morde
Sur mon cœur, parfait instrument,
Et fasse plus royalement
Chanter sa plus vibrante corde,

Que ta voix, chat mystérieux,
Chat séraphique, chat étrange,
En qui tout est, comme en un ange,
Aussi subtil qu'harmonieux!

THE CAT

i

ALONG my brain there walks,
  As though in its own home,
A lovely, strong and sweet and charming cat.
When it mews, one hardly hears,

So tender and discreet its tone;
Appeasing or complaining its voice
Is always rich and deep:
Therein is its charm and secret.

This voice, which glistens and strains
Through the darkest soils of my being,
Satiates me like an harmonious line,
Delights me like a philter.

It lulls to sleep most cruel ills
And holds all ecstasy;
To tell the longest phrase,
It has no need of words.

No, there is no bow that gnaws
On my heart, perfect instrument,
To make more regally sing
The most vibrant string,

Than your voice, mysterious,
Seraphic, strange cat,
In whom all is, like an angel,
As subtle as harmonious!

ii

De sa fourrure blonde et brune
 Sort un parfum si doux, qu'un soir
J'en fus embaumé, pour l'avoir
Caressée une fois, rien qu'une.

C'est l'esprit familier du lieu;
Il juge, il préside, il inspire
Toutes choses dans son empire;
Peut-être est-il fée, est-il dieu?

Quand mes yeux, vers ce chat que j'aime
Tirés comme par un aimant,
Se retournent docilement
Et que je regarde en moi-même,

Je vois avec étonnement
Le feu de ses prunelles pâles,
Clairs fanaux, vivantes opales,
Qui me contemplent fixement.

ii

From its fair and dark fur
Comes a scent so gentle, that one night
I was caught in its balm, by having
Caressed it once, only once.

It is the familiar spirit of the place;
It judges, presides, inspires
Everything in its empire;
It is perhaps a fairy or a god?

When my eyes, drawn like a magnet
To this cat that I love,
Come meekly back again
And I look inside myself,

I see with amazement
The fire of its pale pupils,
Clear beacons, living opals,
Looking at me fixedly.

LE BEAU NAVIRE

JE veux te raconter, ô molle enchanteresse!
  Les diverses beautés qui parent ta jeunesse;
    Je veux te peindre ta beauté,
  Où l'enfance s'allie à la maturité.

Quand tu vas balayant l'air de ta jupe large,
To fais l'effet d'un beau vaisseau qui prend le large,
    Chargé de toile, et va roulant
  Suivant un rhythme doux, et paresseux, et lent.

Sur ton cou large et rond, sur tes épaules grasses,
Ta tête se pavane avec d'étranges grâces;
    D'un air placide et triomphant
  Tu passes ton chemin, majestueuse enfant.

Je veux te raconter, ô molle enchanteresse!
Les diverses beautés qui parent ta jeunesse;
    Je veux te peindre ta beauté,
  Où l'enfance s'allie à la maturité.

Ta gorge qui s'avance et qui pousse la moire,
Ta gorge triomphante est une belle armoire
    Dont les panneaux bombés et clairs
  Comme les boucliers accrochent des éclairs;

Boucliers provoquants, armés de pointes roses!
Armoire à doux secrets, pleine de bonnes choses,
    De vins, de parfums, de liqueurs
  Qui feraient délirer les cerveaux et les cœurs!

Quand tu vas balayant l'air de ta jupe large,
Tu fais l'effet d'un beau vaisseau qui prend le large,
    Chargé de toile, et va roulant
  Suivant un rhythme doux, et paresseux, et lent.

page 60

THE BEAUTIFUL SHIP

I WANT to tell you, indolent enchantress,
Of the various beauties that adorn your youth;
   I want to paint for you your beauty
Of childish maturity.

When you go sweeping the air with your flaring skirts,
You look like a lovely ship taking to flight,
   Heavy with canvas, pitching,
Rolling in a soft rhythm, both lazy and slow.

On your wide, round neck, on your plump shoulders,
Your head parades its strange graces;
   Placidly, triumphantly,
O child of majesty, you go your way.

I want to tell you, indolent enchantress,
Of the various beauties that adorn your youth;
   I want to paint for you your beauty
Where childhood touches maturity.

Your breasts thrust forward, heaving their silk,
Your triumphing breasts are charming cases
   Whose outlined, rounded panels
Hold flashes of light like twin shields;

Provocative shields, armed with pink tips,
Cases of sweet secrets, full of sweet things,
   Of wines and perfumes and liqueurs
Making the brain, the heart delirious!

When you go sweeping the air with your flaring skirts,
You look like a lovely ship taking to flight,
   Heavy with canvas, you go pitching,
Rolling in a soft rhythm, both lazy and slow.

Tes nobles jambes, sous les volants qu'elles chassent,
Tourmentent les désirs obscurs et les agacent,
　　Comme deux sorcières qui font
Tourner un philtre noir dans un vase profond.

Tes bras, qui se joueraient des précoces hercules,
Sont des boas luisants les solides émules,
　　Faits pour serrer obstinément,
Comme pour l'imprimer dans ton cœur, ton amant.

Sur ton cou large et rond, sur tes épaules grasses,
Ta tête se pavane avec d'étranges grâces;
　　D'un air placide et triomphant
Tu passes ton chemin, majestueuse enfant.

Your full legs, under flounces they chase forward,
Torture and excite dark desires,
   Like two witches who
Twist some black potion in a deep bowl.

Your arms, which would make light of precocious Hercules,
Rival well two glistening snakes,
   Made to bind hopelessly
As if to imprison your lover in your heart.

On your wide, round neck, on your plump shoulders,
Your head parades its strange graces
   Placid, triumphantly,
O child of majesty, you go your way.

CAUSERIE

Vous êtes un beau ciel d'automne, clair et rose!
Mais la tristesse en moi monte comme la mer,
Et laisse, en refluant, sur ma lèvre morose
Le souvenir cuisant de son limon amer.

—Ta main se glisse en vain sur mon sein qui se pâme;
Ce qu'elle cherche, amie, est un lieu saccagé
Par la griffe et la dent féroce de la femme.
Ne cherchez plus mon cœur; les bêtes l'ont mangé.

Mon cœur est un palais flétri par la cohue;
On s'y soûle, on s'y tue, on s'y prend aux cheveux!
—Un parfum nage autour de votre gorge nue!...

O Beauté, dur fléau des âmes, tu le veux!
Avec tes yeux de feu, brillants comme des fêtes,
Calcine ces lambeaux qu'ont épargnés les bêtes!

CONVERSATION

YOU are the loveliness, the clearness, the red of autumn
   skies!
But sadness climbs like a sea in me,
Leaving, in reflux, upon my bitter lip
The sharp memory of its biting slime.

—In vain your hand slips on my fainting chest;
What it seeks, my darling, is but a place pillaged
By the fang and the fierce tooth of woman.
Do not search for my heart anymore; the wild beasts have
   eaten it.

My heart is a palace soiled by the mob;
There they swill, and they brawl, and they kill!
—A fragrance swims around your naked breasts. . . .

O Beauty, cruel scourge of souls, you long for it!
With your eyes that flame, brilliant as festivals,
Burn these tatters that the beasts have spared me!

A UNE DAME CREOLE

Au pays parfumé que le soleil caresse,
J'ai connu, sous un dais d'arbres tout empourprés
Et de palmiers d'où pleut sur les yeux la paresse,
Une dame créole aux charmes ignorés.

Son teint est pâle et chaud; la brune enchanteresse
A dans le col des airs noblement maniérés;
Grande et svelte en marchant comme une chasseresse,
Son sourire est tranquille et ses yeux assurés.

Si vous alliez, Madame, au vrai pays de gloire,
Sur les bords de la Seine ou de la verte Loire,
Belle digne d'orner les antiques manoirs,

Vous feriez, à l'abri des ombreuses retraites,
Germer mille sonnets dans le cœur des poètes,
Que vos grands yeux rendraient plus soumis que vos noirs.

TO A CREOLE LADY

IN that perfumed country caressed by the sun,
 I have known, under a canopy of purple trees
And palms raining idleness upon the eyes,
A creole lady of private beauty.

Her shade is pale and warm; this brown enchantress
Has gracefully mannered airs in her neck;
Large and sinuous, walking like a huntress,
Her smile is silent and her eyes secure.

If you should go, Madam, to the true country of glory,
On the banks of the Seine or of the green Loire,
Fair lady fit to decorate ancient mansions,

In some shady and secluded refuge, you would awake
A thousand sonnets in the hearts of poets,
Whom your great eyes would make more subject than
 your Blacks.

LA PIPE

JE suis la pipe d'un auteur;
   On voit, à contempler ma mine
D'Abyssinienne ou de Cafrine,
Que mon maître est un grand fumeur.

Quand il est comblé de douleur,
Je fume comme la chaumine
Où se prépare la cuisine
Pour le retour du laboureur.

J'enlace et je berce son âme
Dans le réseau mobile et bleu
Qui monte de ma bouche en feu,

Et je roule un puissant dictame
Qui charme son cœur et guérit
De ses fatigues son esprit.

THE PIPE

I AM an author's pipe;
From examining my Abyssinian
Or Kaffir countenance, one sees
That my master is a great smoker.

When he is laden with sorrow,
I smoke like a cottage
When the cooking is being prepared
Against the labourer's return.

I entwine and I cradle his soul
In the drifting, blue film
That climbs from my fiery mouth,

And I turn a powerful balm
Which charms his heart and heals
His spirit of fatigues.

LA CLOCHE FELEE

Il est amer et doux, pendant les nuits d'hiver,
 D'écouter, près du feu qui palpite et qui fume
Les souvenirs lointains lentement s'élever
Au bruit des carillons qui chantent dans la brume.

Bienheureuse la cloche au gosier vigoureux
Qui, malgré sa vieillesse, alerte et bien portante,
Jette fidèlement son cri religieux,
Ainsi qu'un vieux soldat qui veille sous la tente!

Moi, mon âme est fêlée, et lorsqu'en ses ennuis
Elle veut de ses chants peupler l'air froid des nuits,
Il arrive souvent que sa voix affaiblie

Semble le râle épais d'un blessé qu'on oublie
Au bord d'un lac de sang, sous un grand tas de morts,
Et qui meurt, sans bouger, dans d'immenses efforts.

THE CRACKED BELL

IT is bitter and sweet, during winter nights,
To listen, beside the throbbing, smoking fire,
To distant memories slowly ascending
In the sound of the chimes chanting through the fog.

Blessed the bell with the vigorous gullet
Which, despite old age, watchful and healthy,
Throws out faithfully its pious tones,
Like an old soldier in vigil under his tent!

Ah, my soul is cracked, and when in sorrows
It wishes to people the cold air of the night with its songs,
Often it happens that its feeble voice

Seems like the thick death-rattle of one wounded, forgotten
By the side of a lake of blood, under a great weight of dead,
Who dies, without moving, amongst enormous efforts.

SPLEEN

Quand le ciel bas et lourd pèse comme un couvercle
   Sur l'esprit gémissant en proie aux longs ennuis,
Et que de l'horizon embrassant tout le cercle
   Il nous verse un jour noir plus triste que les nuits;

Quand la terre est changée en un cachot humide,
   Où l'Espérance, comme une chauve-souris,
S'en va battant les murs de son aile timide
   Et se cognant la tête à des plafonds pourris;

Quand la pluie étalant ses immenses traînées
   D'une vaste prison imite les barreaux,
Et qu'un peuple muet d'infâmes araignées
   Vient tendre ses filets au fond de nos cerveaux,

Des cloches tout à coup sautent avec furie
   Et lancent vers le ciel un affreux hurlement,
Ainsi que des esprits errants et sans patrie
   Qui se mettent à geindre opiniâtrément.

—Et de longs corbillards, sans tambours ni musique,
   Défilent lentement dans mon âme; l'Espoir,
Vaincu, pleure, et l'Angoisse atroce, despotique,
   Sur mon crâne incliné plante son drapeau noir.

SPLEEN

WHEN the low and heavy sky presses like a lid
   On the groaning heart, a prey to slow cares,
And when from a horizon holding the whole orb
There is cast at us a dark sky more sad than night;

When earth is changed to a damp dungeon,
Where Hope, like a bat,
Flees beating the walls with its timorous wings,
And knocking its head on the rotting ceilings;

When the rain spreads out vast trails
Like the bars of a huge prison,
And when, like sordid spiders, silent people stretch
Threads to the depths of our brains,

Suddenly the bells jump furiously
And hurl to the sky a horrible shriek,
Like some wandering landless spirits
Starting an obstinate complaint.

—And long hearses, with no drums, no music,
File slowly through my soul: Hope,
Conquered, cries, and despotic atrocious Agony
Plants on my bent skull its flag of black.

A UNE MENDIANTE ROUSSE

BLANCHE fille aux cheveux roux,
  Dont la robe par ses trous
Laisse voir la pauvreté
  Et la beauté,

Pour moi, poëte chétif,
Ton jeune corps maladif,
Plein de taches de rousseur,
  A sa douceur.

Tu portes plus galamment
Qu'une reine de roman
Ses cothurnes de velours
  Tes sabots lourds.

Au lieu d'un haillon trop court,
Qu'un superbe habit de cour
Traîne à plis bruyants et longs
  Sur tes talons;

En place de bas troués,
Que pour les yeux des roués
Sur ta jambe un poignard d'or
  Reluise encor;

Que des nœuds mal attachés
Dévoilent pour nos péchés
Tex deux beaux seins, radieux
  Comme des yeux;

Que pour te déshabiller
Tex bras se fassent prier
Et chassent à coups mutins
  Les doigts lutins,

TO A RED-HAIRED BEGGAR GIRL

LITTLE white girl with red hair,
   The holes in your frock
Show poverty
   And beauty,

For me, a poor poet,
Your young and ailing body,
Spotted with freckles,
   Has its sweetness.

You carry more gallantly,
Than can a queen of fiction
Her high-boots of velvet,
   Your heavy clogs.

In place of rags too short for you,
May a fine court costume
Be drawn in blustering, long folds
   At your heels;

In place of stockings in holes,
May a dagger of gold
Glitter for the eyes of rakes
   On your leg;

May barely fastened knots
Reveal for our sinning
Your lovely breasts, radiant
   As two eyes;

May, to undress yourself,
Your arms require coaxing
And may they archly repel
   Mischievous fingers,

Perles de la plus belle eau,
Sonnets de maître Belleau
Par tes galants mis aux fers
   Sans cesse offerts,

Valetaille de rimeurs
Te dédiant leurs primeurs
Et contemplant ton soulier
   Sous l'escalier,

Maint page épris du hasard,
Maint seigneur et maint Ronsard
Epieraient pour le déduit
   Ton frais réduit !

Tu compterais dans tes lits
Plus de baisers que de lis
Et rangerais sous tes lois
   Plus d'un Valois !

—Cependant tu vas gueusant
Quelque vieux débris gisant
Au seuil de quelque Véfour
   De carrefour;

Tu vas lorgnant en dessous
Des bijoux de vingt-neuf sous
Dont je ne puis, oh ! pardon !
   Te faire don.

Va donc, sans autre ornement,
Parfum, perles, diamant,
Que ta maigre nudité,
   O ma beauté !

May pearls of finest water,
Sonnets by Belleau,
Be ceaselessly proffered
   By your enslaved lovers,

Trains of servant rhymers,
Dedicating first lines to you
And watching your slipper
   Under the staircase,

Many a flunkey struck at random,
Many a lord and many a Ronsard
Would spy to seduce it
   Your tender retreat!

You would count more kisses
Than lilies in your beds
And you would hold in sway
   More than one Valois!

—Meanwhile you go begging
Some old rubbish lying
On the threshold of some
   Vulgar Véfour;

You go gaping past your shoulder
At twenty-nine sou jewels
Of which, I cannot, I am sorry,
   Make a gift to you.

Go then, without other ornament,
Perfume, pearls or diamonds,
Than your emaciated nudity,
   O my beauty!

A UNE PASSANTE

La rue assourdissante autour de moi hurlait.
Longue, mince, en grand deuil, douleur majestueuse,
Une femme passa, d'une main fastueuse
Soulevant, balançant le feston et l'ourlet;

Agile et noble, avec sa jambe de statue.
Moi, je buvais, crispé comme un extravagant,
Dans son œil, ciel livide où germe l'ouragan,
La douceur qui fascine et le plaisir qui tue.

Un éclair... puis la nuit! – Fugitive beauté
Dont le regard m'a fait soudainement renaître,
Ne te verrai-je plus que dans l'éternité?

Ailleurs, bien loin d'ici! trop tard! *jamais* peut-être!
Car j'ignore où tu fuis, tu ne sais où je vais,
O toi que j'eusse aimée, ô toi qui le savais!

TO A WOMAN PASSING BY

THE deafening road around me roared.
  Tall, slim, in deep mourning, making majestic grief,
A woman passed, lifting and swinging
With a pompous gesture the ornamental hem of her garment,

Swift and noble, with statuesque limb.
As for me, I drank, twitching like an old roué,
From her eye, livid sky where the hurricane is born,
The softness that fascinates and the pleasure that kills.

A gleam ... then night! O fleeting beauty,
Your glance has given me sudden rebirth,
Shall I see you again only in eternity?

Somewhere else, very far from here! Too late! Perhaps never!
For I do not know where you flee, nor you where I am going,
O you whom I would have loved, O you who knew it!

LE CREPUSCULE DU SOIR

VOICI le soir charmant, ami du criminel;
  Il vient comme un complice, à pas de loup; le ciel
Se ferme lentement comme une grande alcôve,
Et l'homme impatient se change en bête fauve.

O soir, aimable soir, désiré par celui
Dont les bras, sans mentir, peuvent dire: Aujourd'hui
Nous avons travaillé! – C'est le soir qui soulage
Les espirits que dévore une douleur sauvage,
Le savant obstiné dont le front s'alourdit,
Et l'ouvrier courbé qui regagne son lit.

Cependant des démons malsains dans l'atmosphère
S'éveillent lourdement, comme des gens d'affaire,
Et cognent en volant les volets et l'auvent.
A travers les lueurs que tourmente le vent
La Prostitution s'allume dans les rues;
Comme une fourmilière elle ouvre ses issues;
Partout elle se fraye un occulte chemin,
Ainsi que l'ennemi qui tente un coup de main;
Elle remue au sein de la cité de fange
Comme un ver qui dérobe à l'Homme ce qu'il mange.
On entend çà et là les cuisines siffler,
Les théâtres glapir, les orchestres ronfler;
Les tables d'hôte, dont le jeu fait les délices,
S'emplissent de catins et d'escrocs, leurs complices,
Et les voleurs, qui n'ont ni trêve ni merci,
Vont bientôt commencer leur travail, eux aussi,
Et forcer doucement les portes et les caisses
Pour vivre quelques jours et vêtir leurs maîtresses.

page 80

EVENING TWILIGHT

NOW is the graceful evening, friend of the criminal;
  Now it comes like an accomplice, stealthily; the sky
Closes slowly like a gigantic bedroom,
And Man, impatient, changes to wild beast.

O evening, lovable eveningtime, longed for by him
Whose arms can truthfully say: Today
We have worked! – It is evening that lightens
Spirits consumed by a fierce sorrow,
The stubborn savant whose forehead grows heavy,
And the bent labourer gaining again his bed.

Meanwhile unhealthy demons heavily awake,
Like business men, in the atmosphere,
And fly and strike the shutters and the awning.
Across those lights the wind tortures
Prostitution is ignited in the streets;
Like an ant-hill she opens her escapes,
Spawning all over a secret path,
Like an enemy's sudden attack;
She stirs on the breast of the city of dung
Like a worm that steals his meals from Man.
Here and there one hears kitchens hissing,
The screaming of theatres and orchestras roaring;
The plain tables, where gambling throws its pleasures,
Fill up with bawds and cheats, accomplices,
And thieves, who know no truce nor grace,
Soon go to get to work, they also,
Depart to force gently safes and doors
For a few days' living and to clothe their mistresses.

Recueille-toi, mon âme, en ce grave moment,
Et ferme ton oreille à ce rugissement.
C'est l'heure où les douleurs des malades s'aigrissent!
La sombre Nuit les prend à la gorge; ils finissent

Leur destinée et vont vers le gouffre commun;
L'hôpital se remplit de leurs soupirs. – Plus d'un
Ne viendra plus chercher la soupe parfumée,
Au coin du feu, le soir, auprès d'une âme aimée.

Encore la plupart n'ont-ils jamais connu
La douceur du foyer et n'ont jamais vécu!

Reflect, O my soul, in this most solemn time,
And close your ears to this roar.
It is the hour when the sorrows of the ill are sharpened.
Dark Night grips them by the throat; they fulfil

Their fate and move into the common whirlpool;
The hospitals are full of their sighing. — More than one
Will no more come back to seek the perfumed soup,
Beside the fire, at night, by a beloved soul.

Still most, most of them have never known
Home's sweetness nor have they really lived.

LE CREPUSCULE DU MATIN

La diane chantait dans les cours des casernes,
Et le vent du matin soufflait sur les lanternes.

C'était l'heure où l'essaim des rêves malfaisants
Tord sur leurs oreillers les bruns adolescents;
Où, comme un œil sanglant qui palpite et qui bouge,
La lampe sur le jour fait une tache rouge;
Où l'âme, sous le poids du corps revêche et lourd,
Imite les combats de la lampe et du jour.
Comme un visage en pleurs que les brises essuient,
L'air est plein du frisson des choses qui s'enfuient,
Et l'homme est las d'écrire et la femme d'aimer.

Les maisons çà et là commençaient à fumer.
Les femmes de plaisir, la paupière livide,
Bouche ouverte, dormaient de leur sommeil stupide;
Les pauvresses, traînant leurs seins maigres et froids,
Soufflaient sur leurs tisons et soufflaient sur leurs doigts.
C'était l'heure où parmi le froid et la lésine
S'aggravent les douleurs des femmes en gésine;
Comme un sanglot coupé par un sang écumeux
Le chant du coq au loin déchirait l'air brumeux;
Une mer de brouillards baignait les édifices,
Et les agonisants dans le fond des hospices
Poussaient leur dernier râle en hoquets inégaux.
Les débauchés rentraient, brisés par leurs travaux.

L'aurore grelottante en robe rose et verte
S'avançait lentement sur la Seine déserte,
Et le sombre Paris, en se frottant les yeux,
Empoignait ses outils, vieillard laborieux.

MORNING TWILIGHT

REVEILLE was blown in the courtyards of barracks,
And the morning wind fanned the lanterns.

It was the hour when those swarms of unwholesome dreams
Twist on their pillows the brown adolescents;
When, like a bloody eye, throbbing and roving,
The lamp marks the day with a red freckle,
When the soul, burdened by the irritable, heavy body,
Copies the struggles of the lamp and the day.
Like a weeping face, wiped by breezes,
The air is filled with quivering of escaping things
And man is tired of writing and woman of loving.

Here and there houses began to smoke.
The ladies of delight, with livid eyelids,
Mouths open, slept their futile sleep;
Pauper women, dragging their thin, cold breasts,
Blew on their brands and blew on their fingers.
It was the hour when in cold and frugality
The pangs of the labouring woman are quickened;
Like a sob sliced by spumy blood
The misty air was slashed by the song of the cock;
A sea of fog bathed the buildings,
And the agonized in the depths of asylums
Uttered their last death-rattles in irregular hiccups.
The debauchees returned, broken by their business.

Dawn, chattering with cold, in its pink and green robe,
Advanced slowly over the deserted Seine,
And grey Paris, rubbing its eyes,
Reached for its tools, like an aged workman.

UNE MARTYRE

Dessin D'un Maître Inconnu

Au milieu des flacons, des étoffes lamées
   Et des meubles voluptueux,
Des marbres, des tableaux, des robes parfumées
   Qui traînent à plis somptueux,

Dans une chambre tiède où, comme en une serre,
   L'air est dangereux et fatal,
Où des bouquets mourants dans leurs cercueils de verre
   Exhalent leur soupir final,

Un cadavre sans tête épanche, comme un fleuve,
   Sur l'oreiller désaltéré
Un sang rouge et vivant, dont la toile s'abreuve
   Avec l'avidité d'un pré.

Semblable aux visions pâles qu'enfante l'ombre
   Et qui nous enchaînent les yeux,
La tête, avec l'amas de sa crinière sombre
   Et de ses bijoux précieux,

Sur la table de nuit, comme une renoncule,
   Repose; et, vide de pensers,
Un regard vague et blanc comme le crépuscule
   S'échappe des yeux révulsés.

Sur le lit, le tronc nu sans scrupules étale
   Dans le plus complet abandon
La secrète splendeur et la beauté fatale
   Dont la nature lui fit don;

Un bas rosâtre, orné de coins d'or, à la jambe
   Comme un souvenir est resté;
La jarretière, ainsi qu'un œil secret qui flambe,
   Darde un regard diamanté.

A MARTYRED WOMAN

Sketch by an Unknown Master

IN the middle of scent-bottles, braided material
   And voluptuous furniture,
Amongst marbles, pictures, perfumed dresses
   Trailing in expensive folds,

In a warm room, where like a hothouse
   The air is dangerous, fatal,
Where dying flowers sigh out their last
   In their glass coffins,

A headless corpse discharges, like a river,
   Upon the slaked pillow,
Its red and living blood, which the linen laps up
   With the greed of a meadow.

Like those ghastly visions engendered by shadows,
   And riveting our eyes
The head, with the weight of its dark mane
   And its precious jewels

Rests like a plant on the bedside table;
   And, empty of thoughts,
A look, loose and white as twilight
   Escapes its misplaced eyes.

On the bed the naked, shameless trunk spreads out
   In utter unconstraint
Its secret splendour and its fatal beauty,
   The gift of nature;

A pink stocking, embroidered with gold sequins, remains
   On the leg like a memory;
The garter, like a flaming, hidden eye,
   Darts a diamonded glance.

Le singulier aspect de cette solitude
  Et d'un grand portrait langoureux,
Aux yeux provocateurs comme son attitude,
  Révèle un amour ténébreux,

Une coupable joie et des fêtes étranges
  Pleines de baisers infernaux,
Dont se réjouissait l'essaim de mauvais anges
  Nageant dans les plis des rideaux;

Et cependant, à voir la maigreur élégante
  De l'épaule au contour heurté,
La hanche un peu pointue et la taille fringante
  Ainsi qu'un reptile irrité,

Elle est bien jeune encor! – Son âme exaspérée
  Et ses sens par l'ennui mordus
S'étaient-ils entr'ouverts à la meute altérée
  Des désirs errants et perdus?

L'homme vindicatif que tu n'as pu, vivante,
  Malgré tant d'amour, assouvir,
Combla-t-il sur ta chair inerte et complaisante
  L'immensité de son désir?

Réponds, cadavre impur! et par tes tresses roides
  Te soulevant d'un bras fiévreux,
Dis-moi, tête effrayante, a-t-il sur tes dents froides,
  Collé les suprêmes adieux?

—Loin du monde railleur, loin de la foule impure,
  Loin des magistrats curieux,
Dors en paix, dors en paix, étrange créature,
  Dans ton tombeau mystérieux;

Ton époux court le monde, et ta forme immortelle
  Veille près de lui quand il dort;
Autant que toi sans doute il te sera fidèle,
  Et constant jusques à la mort.

page 88

The strange look of this solitude
  And of a great languorous tableau,
To eyes provocative as her posture
  Reveals a dark love,

A guilty joy and strange feasts,
  Full of the kisses of hell
That please the swarms of evil angels
  Swimming in the folds of curtains;

And yet, seeing that elegant emaciation
  Of shoulder with the blatant contour
The hip a little angular and the taut waistline
  Like a furious reptile,

She is still quite young! – Did her inflamed soul
  And her senses gnawn by boredom
Yawn for that thirsty pack of
  Wandering, lost passions?

Did that vengeful man whom, living, you could not gratify,
  In spite of so much love
Heap upon your indolent, accommodating flesh
  The size of his desire?

Answer, O violated corpse! and raising yourself with feverish arm
  By your stiff braids,
Tell me, terrifying head, did he press upon your cold teeth
  His final farewells?

—Far from the bantering world, from the corrupted mob,
  Far from inquisitive magistrates,
Sleep peacefully, sleep peacefully, strange creature,
  In your mysterious tomb;

Your husband roves the world and your deathless figure
  Watches by him when he sleeps;
Doubtless he will be faithful as you are,
  And constant to death.

FEMMES DAMNEES

Comme un bétail pensif sur le sable couchées,
Elles tournent leurs yeux vers l'horizon des mers,
Et leurs pieds se cherchant et leurs mains rapprochées
Ont de douces langueurs et des frissons amers.

Les unes, cœurs épris des longues confidences,
Dans le fond des bosquets où jasent les ruisseaux,
Vont épelant l'amour des craintives enfances
Et creusent le bois vert des jeunes arbrisseaux;

D'autres, comme des sœurs, marchent lentes et graves
A travers les rochers pleins d'apparitions,
Où saint Antoine a vu surgir comme des laves
Les seins nus et pourprés de ses tentations;

Il en est, aux lueurs des résines croulantes,
Qui dans le creux muet des vieux antres païens
T'appellent au secours de leurs fièvres hurlantes,
O Bacchus, endormeur des remords anciens!

Et d'autres, dont la gorge aime les scapulaires,
Qui, recélant un fouet sous leurs longs vêtements,
Mêlent, dans le bois sombre et les nuits solitaires,
L'ecume du plaisir aux larmes des tourments.

O vierges, ô démons, ô monstres, ô martyres,
De la réalité grands esprits contempteurs,
Chercheuses d'infini, dévotes et satyres,
Tantôt pleines de cris, tantôt pleines de pleurs,

Vous que dans votre enfer mon âme a poursuivies,
Pauvres sœurs, je vois aime autant que je vous plains,
Pour vos mornes douleurs, vos soifs inassouvies,
Et les urnes d'amour dont vos grands cœurs sont pleins!

THE DAMNED WOMEN

LOUNGING like pensive cattle on the sand,
They turn their eyes to the horizon of seas,
And their feet seek each other and their close hands
Now languish with softness, now quiver with gall.

Some, their hearts captivated by slow secrets
In the depths of bushes chattering with streams,
Go gathering the first loves of timid childhoods
Exploring the green wood of tender trees;

Others, like nuns, slow and grave, move
Over rocks swarming with visions,
Where St. Anthony saw rise up the lava
Of the purple naked breasts of his temptations;

There are some who, to the resin's shaking glimmer,
Call, from the silent hollows of old pagan caverns,
To you, O Bacchus, who soothe remorse,
For help out of their shouting fevers.

And others, whose bosoms crave the scapular,
Who hide a whip under their long clothes
And mingle, in the dismal wood and lonely night,
The foam of pleasure with the twists of pain.

To you, virgins, demons, monsters, martyrs,
To your great spirits spurning reality,
Searchers of the infinite, devotees and satyrs,
Now full of cries, now full of tears,

To you whom to your hell my soul has followed
My poor sisters, I give you my love and pity,
For your dark sorrows, your unslakeable thirsts,
And the caskets of your love of which your hearts are full!

LA FIN DE LA JOURNEE

SOUS une lumière blafarde
   Court, danse et se tord sans raison
La Vie, impudente et criarde,
Aussi, sitôt qu'à l'horizon

La nuit voluptueuse monte,
Apaisant tout, même la faim,
Effaçant tout, même la honte,
Le Poëte se dit: 'Enfin!

'Mon esprit, comme mes vertèbres,
Invoque ardemment le repos;
Le cœur plein de songes funèbres,

'Je vais me coucher sur le dos
Et me rouler dans vos rideaux,
O rafraîchissantes ténèbres!'

THE END OF THE DAY

UNDER a sallow light
   Runs insolent, shrieking Life,
Dancing and twisting capriciously.
Then, as soon as sensual night

Climbs the horizon
Hushing all, even hunger,
Effacing all, even shame,
The Poet says to himself: 'At last

My spirit like my bones
Pleads dearly for repose;
My heart is full of melancholy dreams,

And I go and lie on my back
Coiling myself in your curtains,
O restoring darkness!'

LE VOYAGE

A Maxime du Camp

i

POUR l'enfant, amoureux de cartes et d'estampes,
  L'univers est égal à son vaste appétit.
Ah! que le monde est grand à la clarté des lampes!
Aux yeux du souvenir que le monde est petit!

Un matin nous partons, le cerveau plein de flamme,
Le cœur gros de rancune et de désirs amers,
Et nous allons, suivant le rhythme de la lame,
Berçant notre infini sur le fini des mers:

Les uns, joyeux de fuir une patrie infâme;
D'autres, l'horreur de leurs berceaux, et quelques-uns,
Astrologues noyés dans les yeux d'une femme,
La Circé tyrannique aux dangereux parfums.

Pour n'être pas changés en bêtes, ils s'enivrent
D'espace et de lumière et de cieux embrasés;
La glace qui les mord, les soleils qui les cuivrent,
Effacent lentement la marque des baisers.

Mais les vrais voyageurs sont ceux-là seuls qui partent
Pour partir; cœurs légers, semblables aux ballons,
De leur fatalité jamais ils ne s'écartent,
Et, sans savoir pourquoi, disent toujours: Allons!

Ceux-là dont les désirs ont la forme des nues,
Et qui rêvent, ainsi qu'un conscrit le canon,
De vastes voluptés, changeantes, inconnues
Et dont l'esprit humain n'a jamais su le nom!

THE JOURNEY

To Maxime du Camp

i

For the child, adoring cards and prints,
  The universe fulfils its vast appetite.
Ah, how large is the world in the brightness of lamps,
How small in the eyes of memory!

We leave one morning, brains full of flame,
Hearts full of malice and bitter desires,
And we go and follow the rhythm of the waves,
Rocking our infinite on the finite of the seas:

Some happy to escape a tainted country
Others, the horrors of their cradles; and a few,
Astrologers drowned in the eyes of a woman,
Some tyrannical Circe of dangerous perfumes.

So not to be transformed into animals, they get drunk
On space and light and skies on fire;
The biting ice, the suns that turn them copper,
Slowly blot out the brand of kisses.

But the true travellers are they who depart
For departing's sake; with hearts light as balloons,
They never swerve from their destinies,
Saying continuously, without knowing why: 'Let us go on!'

These have passions formed like clouds;
As a recruit of his gun, they dream
Of spacious pleasures, transient, little understood,
Whose name no human spirit knows.

ii

Nous imitons, horreur! la toupie et la boule
Dans leur valse et leurs bonds; même dans nos sommeils
La Curiosité nous tourmente et nous roule,
Comme un Ange cruel qui fouette des soleils.

Singulière fortune, où le but se déplace,
Et, n'étant nulle part, peut être n'importe où!
Où l'Homme, dont jamais l'espérance n'est lasse,
Pour trouver le repos court toujours comme un fou!

Notre âme est un trois-mâts cherchant son Icarie;
Une voix retentit sur le pont: 'Ouvre l'œil!'
Une voix de la hune, ardente et folle, crie:
'Amour...gloire...bonheur!' Enfer! c'est un écueil.

Chaque îlot signalé par l'homme de vigie
Est un Eldorado promis par le Destin;
L'Imagination qui dresse son orgie
Ne trouve qu'un récif aux clartés du matin.

O le pauvre amoureux des pays chimériques!
Faut-il mettre aux fers, le jeter à la mer,
Ce matelot ivrogne, inventeur d'Amériques
Dont le mirage rend le gouffre plus amer?

Tel le vieux vagabond, piétinant dans la boue,
Rêve, le nez en l'air, de brillants paradis;
Son œil ensorcelé découvre une Capoue
Partout où la chandelle illumine un taudis.

ii

It is a terrible thought that we imitate
The top and the ball in their bounding waltzes; even asleep
Curiosity tortures and turns us
Like a cruel angel whipping the sun.

Whimsical fortune, whose end is out of place
And, being nowhere, can be anywhere!
Where Man, in whom Hope is never weary,
Runs ever like a madman searching for repose.

Our soul is a brigantine seeking its Icaria;
A voice resounds on deck: 'Open your eyes!'
A hot mad voice from the maintop cries:
'Love ... glory ... fortune!' Hell is a rock.

Each little island sighted by the look-out man
Becomes another Eldorado, the promise of Destiny;
Imagination, setting out its revels,
Finds but a reef in the morning light.

O the poor lover of chimerical lands!
Must one put him in irons, throw him in the water,
This drunken sailor, contriver of those Americas
Whose glimpses make the gulfs more bitter?

Thus the old vagabond, tramping through the mud,
With his nose in the air, dreams of shining Edens;
Bewitched his eye finds a Capua
Wherever a candle glimmers in a hovel.

iii

Etonnants voyageurs! quelles nobles histoires
Nous lisons dans vos yeux profonds còmme les mers!
Montrez-nous les écrins de vos riches mémoires,
Ces bijoux merveilleux, faits d'astres et d'éthers.

Nous voulons voyager sans vapeur et sans voile!
Faites, pour égayer l'ennui de nos prisons,
Passer sur nos esprits, tendus comme une toile,
Vos souvenirs avec leurs cadres d'horizons.

Dites, qu'avez-vous vu?

iii

O marvellous travellers! what glorious stories
We read in your eyes as deep as the seas.
Show us the caskets of your rich memories
Those wonderful jewels of stars and stratosphere.

We would travel without wind or sail!
And so, to gladden the cares of our jails,
Pass over our spirits, stretched out like canvas,
Your memories with their frames of horizons.

Tell us, what have you seen?

iv

'Nous avons vu des astres
Et des flots; nous avons vu des sables aussi;
Et, malgré bien des chocs et d'imprévus désastres,
Nous nous sommes souvent ennuyés, comme ici.

'La gloire du soleil sur la mer violette,
La gloire des cités dans le soleil couchant,
Allumaient dans nos cœurs une ardeur inquiète
De plonger dans un ciel au reflet alléchant.

'Les plus riches cités, les plus grands paysages,
Jamais ne contenaient l'attrait mystérieux
De ceux que le hasard fait avec les nuages,
Et toujours le désir nous rendait soucieux!

'—La jouissance ajoute au désir de la force.
Désir, vieil arbre à qui le plaisir sert d'engrais,
Cependant que grossit et durcit ton écorce,
Tes branches veulent voir le soleil de plus près!

'Grandiras-tu toujours, grand arbre plus vivace
Que le cyprès? – Pourtant nous avons, avec soin,
Cueilli quelques croquis pour votre album vorace,
Frères qui trouvez beau tout ce qui vient de loin!

'Nous avons salué des idoles à trompe,
Des trônes constellés de joyaux lumineux;
Des palais ouvragés dont la féerique pompe
Serait pour vos banquiers un rêve ruineux;

'Des costumes qui sont pour les yeux une ivresse;
Des femmes dont les dents et les ongles sont teints,
Et des jongleurs savants que le serpent caresse.'

iv

'We have seen the stars
And the waves; and we have seen the sands also;
And, despite shocks and unforeshadowed disasters,
We have often, as here, grown weary.

The glory of sunlight on the violet sea,
The glory of cities in the setting sun,
Lit in our hearts an uneasy desire
To sink in a sky of enticing reflections.

Never did the richest cities, the grandest countryside,
Hold such mysterious charms
As those chance made amongst the clouds,
And ever passion made us anxious!

—Delight adds power to desire.
O desire, you old tree, your pasture is pleasure,
And whilst your bark grows great and hard
Your branches long to see the sun close to!

Do you ever increase, grand tree, you who live
Longer than the cypress? – Nevertheless, we have carefully
Culled some sketches for your ravenous album,
Brothers finding beauty in all things coming from afar!

We have greeted great horned idols,
Thrones starry with luminous jewels,
Figured palaces whose fairy pomp
Would be a dream of ruin for a banker,

Robes which make the eyes intoxicated;
Women with tinted teeth and nails
And cunning jugglers caressed by serpents.'

Et puis, et puis encore?

vi

'O cerveaux enfantins!

'Pour ne pas oublier la chose capitale,
Nous avons vu partout, et sans l'avoir cherché,
Du haut jusques en bas de l'échelle fatale,
Le spectacle ennuyeux de l'immortel péché:

'La femme, esclave vile, orgueilleuse et stupide,
Sans rire s'adorant et s'aimant sans dégoût;
L'homme, tyran goulu, paillard, dur et cupide,
Esclave de l'esclave et ruisseau dans l'égout;

'Le bourreau qui jouit, le martyre qui sanglote;
La fête qu'assaisonne et parfume le sang;
Le poison du pouvoir énervant le despote,
Et le peuple amoureux du fouet abrutissant;

'Plusieurs religions semblables à la nôtre,
Toutes escaladant le ciel; la Sainteté,
Comme en un lit de plume un délicat se vautre,
Dans les clous et le crin cherchant la volupté;

'L'Humanité bavarde, ivre de son génie,
Et, folle maintenant comme elle était jadis,
Criant à Dieu, dans sa furibonde agonie:
"O mon semblable, ô mon maître, je te maudis!"

'Et les moins sots, hardis amants de la Démence,
Fuyant le grand troupeau parqué par le Destin,
Et se réfugiant dans l'opium immense!
—Tel est du globe entier l'éternel bulletin.'

page 102

v

And then, what then?

vi

'O childish minds!

Never to forget the principal matter,
We have everywhere seen, without having sought it,
From top to bottom of the fatal ladder,
The wearisome spectacle of immortal sin:

Woman, base slave of pride and stupidity,
Adores herself without a smile, loves herself with no distaste;
Man, that gluttonous, lewd tyrant, hard and avaricious,
Is a slave of the slave, a trickle in the sewer;

The joyful executioner, the sobbing martyr;
The festival that flavours and perfumes the blood;
The poisonous power that weakens the oppressor
And the people craving the agonizing whip;

Many religions like ours
All scaling the heavens; Sanctity
Like a tender voluptuary wallowing in a feather bed
Seeking sensuality in nails and horse-hair;

Prating Humanity, besotted with its own genius,
Is as mad today as ever it was,
Crying to God in its furious agony:
"O my fellow and my master, I curse thee!"

And the less senseless, brave lovers of Dementia,
Flee the great herd penned in by Destiny,
And take refuge in a vast opium!
—Such is the eternal report of the whole world.'

vii

Amer savoir, celui qu'on tire du voyage!
Le monde, monotone et petit, aujourd'hui,
Hier, demain, toujours, nous fait voir notre image;
Une oasis d'horreur dans un désert d'ennui!

Faut-il partir? Si tu peux rester, reste;
Pars, s'il le faut. L'un court, et l'autre se tapit
Pour tromper l'ennemi vigilant et funeste,
Le Temps! Il est, hélas! des coureurs sans répit,

Comme le Juif errant et comme les apôtres,
A qui rien ne suffit, ni wagon, ni vaisseau,
Pour fuir ce rétiaire infâme; il en est d'autres
Qui savent le tuer sans quitter leur berceau.

Lorsque enfin il mettra le pied sur notre échine,
Nous pourrons espérer et crier: En avant!
De même qu'autrefois nous partions pour la Chine,
Les yeux fixés au large et les cheveux au vent,

Nous nous embarquerons sur la mer des Ténèbres
Avec le cœur joyeux d'un jeune passager.
Entendez-vous ces voix, charmantes et funèbres,
Qui chantent: 'Par ici! vous qui voulez manger

'Le Lotus parfumé! c'est ici qu'on vendange
Les fruits miraculeux dont votre cœur a faim;
Venez vous enivrer de la douceur étrange
De cette après-midi qui n'a jamais de fin!'

A l'accent familier nous devinons le spectre;
Nos Pylades là-bas tendent leurs bras vers nous.
'Pour rafraîchir ton cœur nage vers ton Electre!'
Dit celle dont jadis nous baisions les genoux.

page 104

vii

O bitter is the knowledge that one draws from the voyage!
The monotonous and tiny world, today
Yesterday, tomorrow, always, shows us our reflections,
An oasis of horror in a desert of boredom!

Must we depart? If you can do so, remain;
Depart, if you must. Someone runs, another crouches,
To deceive that vigilant and fatal enemy,
Time! Ah, there are some runners who know no respite,

Like the wandering Jew or like the apostles,
Whom nothing aids, no cart, nor ship,
To flee this ugly gladiator; there are others
Who even in their cradles know how to kill it.

When at last he shall place his foot upon our spine,
We will be capable of hope, crying: 'Forward!'
As in old times we left for China,
Eyes fixed in the distance, hair in the winds,

We shall embark on that sea of Darkness
With the happy heart of a young traveller.
Do you hear these voices, alluring and funereal,
Singing: 'This way, those of you who long to eat

The perfumed lotus-leaf! it is here that are gathered
Those miraculous fruits for which your heart hungers;
Do come and get drunk on the strange sweetness
Of this afternoon without end!'

By those familiar accents we discover the phantom
Over there our personal Pylades stretch out their arms to us.
'Swim to your Electra to revive your hearts!'
Says she whose knees we one time kissed.

viii

O Mort, vieux capitaine, il est temps! levons l'ancre!
Ce pays nous ennuie, ô Mort! Appareillons!
Si le ciel et la mer sont noirs comme de l'encre,
Nos cœurs que tu connais sont remplis de rayons!

Verse-nous ton poison pour qu'il nous réconforte!
Nous voulons, tant ce feu nous brûle le cerveau,
Plonger au fond du gouffre, Enfer ou Ciel, qu'importe?
Au fond de l'Inconnu pour trouver du *nouveau*!

viii

O Death, my captain, it is time! let us raise the anchor!
This country wearies us, O Death! Let us make ready!
If sea and sky are both as black as ink,
You know our hearts are full of sunshine.

Pour on us your poison to refresh us!
Oh, this fire so burns our brains, we would
Dive to the depths of the gulf, Heaven or Hell, what matter?
If only to find in the depths of the Unknown the New!

LE LETHE

VIENS sur mon cœur, âme cruelle et sourde,
    Tigre adoré, monstre aux airs indolents;
Je veux longtemps plonger mes doigts tremblants
Dans l'épaisseur de ta crinière lourde;

Dans tes jupons remplis de ton parfum
Ensevelir ma tête endolorie,
Et respirer, comme une fleur flétrie,
Le doux relent de mon amour défunt.

Je veux dormir! dormir plutôt que vivre!
Dans un sommeil aussi doux que la mort,
J'étalerai mes baisers sans remord
Sur ton beau corps poli comme le cuivre.

Pour engloutir mes sanglots apaisés
Rien ne me vaut l'abîme de ta couche;
L'oubli puissant habite sur ta bouche,
Et le Léthé coule dans tes baisers.

A mon destin, désormais mon délice,
J'obéirai comme un prédestiné;
Martyr docile, innocent condamné,
Dont la ferveur attise le supplice,

Je sucerai, pour noyer ma rancœur,
Le népenthès et la bonne ciguë
Aux bouts charmants de cette gorge aiguë,
Qui n'a jamais emprisonné de cœur.

LETHE

COME on my heart, cruel and insensible soul,
My darling tiger, beast with indolent airs;
I want to plunge for hours my trembling fingers
In your thick and heavy mane;

In your petticoats filled with your perfume
To bury my aching head,
And breathe, like a faded flower,
The sweet taste of my dead love.

I want to sleep, to sleep and not to live,
In a sleep as soft as death,
I shall cover with remorseless kisses
Your body beautifully polished as copper.

To swallow my appeased sobbing
I need only the abyss of your bed;
A powerful oblivion lives on your lips,
And all Lethe flows in your kisses.

I shall obey, as though predestined,
My destiny, that is now my delight;
Submissive martyr, innocent damned one,
My ardour inflames my torture,

And I shall suck, to drown my bitterness
The nepenthe and the good hemlock,
On the lovely tips of those jutting breasts
Which have never imprisoned love.

A CELLE QUI EST TROP GAIE

Ta tête, ton geste, ton air
  Sont beaux comme un beau paysage;
Le rire joue en ton visage
Comme un vent frais dans un ciel clair.

Le passant chagrin que tu frôles
Est ébloui par la santé
Qui jaillit comme une clarté
De tes bras et de tes épaules.

Les retentissantes couleurs
Dont tu parsèmes tes toilettes
Jettent dans l'esprit des poëtes
L'image d'un ballet de fleurs.

Ces robes folles sont l'emblème
De ton esprit bariolé;
Folle dont je suis affolé,
Je te hais autant que je t'aime!

Quelquefois dans un beau jardin
Où je traînais mon atonie,
J'ai senti, comme une ironie,
Le soleil déchirer mon sein;

Et le printemps et la verdure
Ont tant humilié mon cœur,
Que j'ai puni sur une fleur
L'insolence de la Nature.

Ainsi, je voudrais, une nuit,
Quand l'heure des voluptés sonne,
Vers les trésors de ta personne,
Comme un lâche, ramper sans bruit,

TO HER WHO IS TOO GAY

YOUR head, your gesture, your air
  Are beautiful as a beautiful landscape;
The smile plays in your face
Like a fresh wind in a clear sky.

The fleeting care that you brush against
Is dazzled by the health
Which leaps like clarity
From your arms and your shoulders.

The re-echoing colours
Which you scatter in your toilet
Cast in the hearts of poets
The image of a ballet of flowers.

These silly clothes are the emblem
Of your many-coloured spirit;
Silly woman of my infatuation,
I hate as much as love you!

Sometimes in a pretty garden
Where I dragged my weakness,
I have felt the sun like irony
Tear my chest;

And the spring and the green of things
Have so humbled my heart,
That I have punished a flower
For the insolence of Nature.

Thus I would wish, one night,
When the voluptuary's hour sounds,
To crawl like a coward, noiselessly,
Towards the treasures of your body,

Pour châtier ta chair joyeuse,
Pour meurtrir ton sein pardonné,
Et faire à ton flanc étonné
Une blessure large et creuse,

Et, vertigineuse douceur!
A travers ces lèvres nouvelles,
Plus éclatantes et plus belles,
T'infuser mon venin, ma sœur!

In order to correct your gay flesh
And beat your unbegrudging breast,
To make upon your starting thigh
A long and biting weal,

And, sweet giddiness,
Along those newly-gaping lips
More vivid and more beautiful,
Inject my venom, O my sister!

LES METAMORPHOSES DU VAMPIRE

La femme cependant, de sa bouche de fraise,
En se tordant ainsi qu'un serpent sur la braise,
Et pétrissant ses seins sur le fer de son busc,
Laissait couler ces mots tout imprégnés de musc:
—'Moi, j'ai la lèvre humide, et je sais la science
De perdre au fond d'un lit l'antique conscience.
Je sèche tous les pleurs sur mes seins triomphants
Et fais rire les vieux du rire des enfants.
Je remplace, pour qui me voit nue et sans voiles,
La lune, le soleil, le ciel et les étoiles!
Je suis, mon cher savant, si docte aux voluptés,
Lorsque j'étouffe un homme en mes bras redoutés,
Ou lorsque j'abandonne aux morsures mon buste,
Timide et libertine, et fragile et robuste,
Que sur ces matelas qui se pâment d'émoi,
Les anges impuissants se damneraient pour moi!'

Quand elle eut de mes os sucé toute la moelle,
Et que languissamment je me tournai vers elle
Pour lui rendre un baiser d'amour, je ne vis plus
Qu'une outre aux flancs gluants, toute pleine de pus!
Je fermai les deux yeux, dans ma froide épouvante,
Et quand je les rouvris à la clarté vivante,
A mes côtés, au lieu du mannequin puissant
Qui semblait avoir fait provision de sang,
Tremblaient confusément des débris de squelette,
Qui d'eux-mêmes rendaient le cri d'une girouette
Ou d'une enseigne, au bout d'une tringle de fer,
Que balance le vent pendant les nuits d'hiver.

THE METAMORPHOSES OF THE VAMPIRE

THEN the woman with the strawberry mouth,
 Squirming like a snake upon the coals,
Kneading her breasts against the iron of her corset,
Let flow these words scented with musk:
—'I have wet lips, and I know the art
Of losing old conscience in the depths of a bed.
I dry all tears on my triumphing breasts
And I make old men laugh with the laughter of children.
For those who see me naked, without any covering,
I am the moon and the sun and the sky and the stars!
I am so dexterous in voluptuous love, my dear, my wise one,
When I strangle a man in my dreadful arms,
Or abandon my breast to his biting,
So shy and lascivious, so frail and vigorous,
That on these cushions that swoon with passion
The powerless angels damn their souls for me!'

When she had sucked the pith from my bones
And, drooping, I turned towards her
To give her the kiss of love, I saw only
An old leather bottle with sticky sides and full of pus!
I shut both eyes in cold dismay
And when I opened them both to clear reality,
By my side, instead of that powerful puppet
Which seemed to have taken some lease of blood,
There shook vaguely the remains of a skeleton,
Which itself gave the cry of a weathercock
Or of a sign-board, at the end of a rod of iron,
Which the wind swings in winter nights.

LES YEUX DE BERTHE

VOUS pouvez mépriser les yeux les plus célèbres,
  Beaux yeux de mon enfant, par où filtre et s'enfuit
Je ne sais quoi de bon, de doux comme la Nuit!
Beaux yeux, versez sur moi vos charmantes ténèbres!

Grands yeux de mon enfant, arcanes adorés,
Vous ressemblez beaucoup à ces grottes magiques
Où, derrière l'amas des ombres léthargiques,
Scintillent vaguement des trésors ignorés!

Mon enfant a des yeux obscurs, profonds et vastes,
Comme toi, Nuit immense, éclairés comme toi!
Leurs feux sont ces pensers d'Amour, mêlés de Foi,
Qui pétillent au fond, voluptueux ou chastes.

THE EYES OF MY CHILD

YOU can despise the most celebrated eyes,
  O eyes of my lovely child, through which filter and flee
The goodness and softness of Night immeasurably!
Beautiful eyes, pour on me your charming darkness!

Great eyes of my child, adorable mysteries,
You look so like those magical grottos
Where, from heaps of lethargic shadows,
Dimly sparkle unknown treasures!

My child has dark, deep eyes and wide,
Illuminated like you, like you, enormous night!
Their fires are dreams of Love and Faith
Scintillating in the very heart, voluptuous or chaste.

HYMNE

A LA très-chère, à la très-belle
Qui remplit mon cœur de clarté,
A l'ange, à l'idole immortelle,
Salut en immortalité !

Elle se répand dans ma vie
Comme un air imprégné de sel,
Et dans mon âme inassouvie
Verse le goût de l'éternel.

Sachet toujours frais qui parfume
L'atmosphère d'un cher réduit,
Encensoir oublié qui fume
En secret à travers la nuit,

Comment, amour incorruptible,
T'exprimer avec vérité ?
Grain de musc qui gis, invisible,
Au fond de mon éternité !

A la très-bonne, à la très-belle
Qui fait ma joie et ma santé,
A l'ange, à l'idole immortelle,
Salut en immortalité !

HYMN

To the most dear, to the most beautiful
   Who fills my heart with brightness,
To the angel, to the immortal idol
Salute to immortality!

She diffuses through my life
Like air alive with brine,
And in my insatiated soul
Pours the flavour of eternity.

Sachet ever fresh that perfumes
The atmosphere of a dear room
Forgotten censer smoking
Secretly across the night,

How, O imperishable love,
Can I express you truly?
Grain of musk lying invisibly
In the depths of my eternity!

To the most good, to the most beautiful
Who is my joy and welfare,
To the angel, to the immortal idol
Salute to immortality!

LES PROMESSES D'UN VISAGE

J'AIME, ô pâle beauté, tes sourcils surbaissés,
  D'où semblent couler des ténèbres;
Tes yeux, quoique très-noirs, m'inspirent des pensers
  Qui ne sont pas du tout funèbres.

Tes yeux, qui sont d'accord avec tes noirs cheveux,
  Avec ta crinière élastique,
Tes yeux languissamment, me disent: 'Si tu veux,
  Amant de la muse plastique,

Suivre l'espoir qu'en toi nous avons excité,
  Et tous les goûts que tu professes,
Tu pourras constater notre véracité
  Depuis le nombril jusqu'aux fesses;

Tu trouveras au bout de deux beaux seins bien lourds,
  Deux larges médailles de bronze,
Et sous un ventre uni, doux comme du velours,
  Bistré comme la peau d'un bonze,

Une riche toison qui, vraiment, est la sœur
  De cette énorme chevelure,
Souple et frisée, et qui t'égale en épaisseur,
  Nuit sans étoiles, Nuit obscure!'

THE PROMISES OF A FACE

I LOVE your elliptical eyebrows, my pale beauty,
  From which darkness seems to flow;
Although so black, your eyes suggest to me
  Thoughts in no way funereal.

Your eyes, in harmony with your black hair,
  With your buoyant mane,
Your swooning eyes now tell me: 'If you wish,
  O lover of the plastic muse,

To follow the hope we have excited in you,
  And all the fancies you profess,
You will be able to prove our truthfulness
  From the navel to the buttocks;

You will find at the tips of two heavy breasts
  Two slack bronze medallions,
And under a smooth belly, soft as velvet,
  Swarthy as the skin of a Buddhist,

A rich fleece, which truly is the sister
  Of this huge head of hair,
Compliant and curly, its thickness equals
  Black night, night without stars!'

A UNE MALABARAISE

Tes pieds sont aussi fins que tes mains, et ta hanche
  Est large à faire envie à la plus belle blanche;
A l'artiste pensif ton corps est doux et cher;
Tes grands yeux de velours sont plus noirs que ta chair.
Aux pays chauds et bleus où ton Dieu t'a fait naître,
Ta tâche est d'allumer la pipe de ton maître,
De pourvoir les flacons d'eaux fraîches et d'odeurs,
De chasser loin du lit les moustiques rôdeurs,
Et, dès que le matin fait chanter les platanes,
D'acheter au bazar ananas et bananes.
Tout le jour, où tu veux, tu mènes tes pieds nus,
Et fredonnes tout bas de vieux airs inconnus;
Et quand descend le soir au manteau d'écarlate,
Tu poses doucement ton corps sur une natte,
Où tes rêves flottants sont pleins de colibris,
Et toujours, comme toi, gracieux et fleuris.

Pourquoi, l'heureuse enfant, veux-tu voir notre France,
Ce pays trop peuplé que fauche la souffrance,
Et, confiant ta vie aux bras forts des marins,
Faire de grands adieux à tes chers tamarins?
Toi, vêtue à moitié de mousselines frêles,
Frissonnante là-bas sous la neige et les grêles,
Comme tu pleurerais tes loisirs doux et francs,
Si, le corset brutal emprisonnant tes flancs,
Il te fallait glaner ton souper dans nos fanges
Et vendre le parfum de tes charmes étranges,
L'œil pensif, et suivant, dans nos sales brouillards,
Des cocotiers absents les fantômes épars!

TO A LADY OF MALABAR

YOUR feet are slim as your hands, and your hips
   Are the heavy envy of the most beautiful white woman;
To the thoughtful artist your body is soft and lovable;
Your great velvet eyes are darker than your skin.
In the warm blue climate where your God bore you,
Your task is to light the pipe of your master,
To keep the flasks of fresh water and spices,
To drive far from the bed raiding mosquitoes
And, when the plane-trees sing in the morning,
To buy pine-apples and bananas at the bazaar.
All day long anywhere you lead your naked feet,
To low humming of old unknown tunes;
And when the scarlet cloak of evening drops
Softly you place your body on a mat,
Your floating dreams are full of humming birds,
Ever, like you, graceful and flowering.

O why, happy child, do you want to see our France,
That populous country slashed by suffering,
To confide your life to the arms of strong sailors,
Bidding last farewells to your darling tamarind-trees?
There, clad in sleazy muslin,
Shivering in the snow and hailstorms,
How you would cry for your sweet free playtimes
If, with the cruel corset clasping your breasts,
You had to glean your supper from our mud,
To trade the perfume of your foreign charms
With your pensive eyes seeking amongst our dirty fogs
The slender ghosts of distant coco-palms!

RECUEILLEMENT

Sois sage, ô ma Douleur, et tiens-toi plus tranquille.
Tu réclamais le Soir; il descend; le voici:
Une atmosphère obscure enveloppe la ville,
Aux uns portant la paix, aux autres le souci.

Pendant que des mortels la multitude vile,
Sous le fouet du Plaisir, ce bourreau sans merci,
Va cueillir des remords dans la fête servile,
Ma Douleur, donne-moi la main; viens par ici,

Loin d'eux. Vois se pencher les défuntes Années,
Sur les balcons du ciel, en robes surannées;
Surgir du fond des eaux le Regret souriant;

Le Soleil moribond s'endormir sous une arche;
Et, comme un long linceul traînant à l'Orient,
Entends, ma chère, entends la douce Nuit qui marche.

MEDITATION

BE wise, O my Sorrow, be calmer.
 You implored the evening; it falls; here it is:
A dusky air surrounds the town,
Bringing peace to some, worry to others.

Whilst the worthless crowd of humanity,
Lashed by Pleasure, that merciless torturer,
Go to gather remorse in slavish rejoicing,
Give me your hand, my Sorrow; come with me,

Far from them. See the dead years leaning,
In worn-out clothing, on the balconies of the skies;
See how Regret, grinning, rises from the deep waters;

The dying sun goes to sleep in an archway,
And, like a long shroud dragging from the East,
Hear, O my dear one, hear the soft night coming.

LES PLAINTES D'UN ICARE

Les amants des prostituées
    Sont heureux, dispos et repus;
Quant à moi, mes bras sont rompus
Pour avoir étreint des nuées.

C'est grâce aux astres nonpareils,
Qui tout au fond du ciel flamboient,
Que mes yeux consumés ne voient
Que des souvenirs de soleils.

En vain j'ai voulu de l'espace
Trouver la fin et le milieu;
Sous je ne sais quel œil de feu
Je sens mon aile qui se casse;

Et brûlé par l'amour du beau,
Je n'aurai pas l'honneur sublime
De donner mon nom a l'abîme
Qui me servira de tombeau.

THE LAMENTATIONS OF AN ICARUS

THE lovers of prostitutes are
  Happy, cheerful, well-fed;
As for me, my arms are broken
Through having hugged the clouds.

It is thanks to the incomparable stars,
Blazing in the depths of the sky,
That my devoured eyes see only
The memories of suns.

In vain I wished to find
The centre and the end of space;
I know not under what fiery eye
I feel my wings breaking;

And burnt up by love of beauty,
I shall not have the splendid honour
Of giving my name to the abyss
Which will serve as my grave.

Selected Grove Press Paperbacks

B181	ANONYMOUS / A Man With A Maid / $2.25
B383	ARSAN, EMMANUELLE / Emmanuelle II / $2.95
E96	BECKETT, SAMUEL / Endgame / $1.95
B78	BECKETT, SAMUEL / Three Novels (Molloy, Malone Dies, The Unnamable) / $3.95
E33	BECKETT, SAMUEL / Waiting For Godot / $1.95
B108	BRECHT, BERTOLT / Mother Courage and Her Children / $1.95
B115	BURROUGHS, WILLIAM S. / Naked Lunch / $2.95
E773	CLURMAN, HAROLD (Ed.) / Nine Plays of the Modern Theater / $9.50 (Waiting For Godot by Samuel Beckett, The Visit by Friedrich Dürrenmatt, Tango by Slavomir Hrozek, The Caucasian Chalk Circle by Bertolt Brecht, The Balcony by Jean Genet, Rhinoceros by Eugene Ionesco, American Buffalo by David Mamet, The Birthday Party by Harold Pinter and Rosencrantz and Guildenstern are Dead by Tom Stoppard)
B342	FANON, FRANTZ / The Wretched of the Earth / $2.45
E130	GENET, JEAN / The Balcony / $2.95
E208	GENET, JEAN / The Blacks: A Clown Show / $3.95
E101	IONESCO, EUGENE / Four Plays (The Bald Soprano, The Lesson, The Chairs, and Jack, or The Submission) / $2.95
E259	IONESCO, EUGENE / Rhinoceros and Other Plays / $2.95
B276	KRONHAUSEN, DRS. PHYLLIS AND EBERHARD / Erotic Fantasies: A Study of the Sexual Imagination / $3.95
B373	LUCAS, GEORGE / American Graffiti / $1.75
B10	MILLER, HENRY / Tropic of Cancer / $2.50
B59	MILLER, HENRY / Tropic of Capricorn / $1.95
E770	NELSON, PAUL / Rod Stewart: A Biography / $8.95
E411	PINTER, HAROLD / The Homecoming / $2.45
B438	REAGE, PAULINE / The Story of O, Part II: Return to the Chateau / $2.25
E759	ROBERTS, RANDY / Jack Dempsey: The Manassa Mauler / $6.95
E618	SNOW, EDGAR / Red Star Over China / $4.95
B319	STOPPARD, TOM / Rosencrantz and Guildenstern Are Dead / $1.95
B341	SUZUKI, D. T. / An Introduction to Zen Buddhism / $1.95

GROVE PRESS, INC., 196 West Houston St., New York, N.Y. 10014